THE CHALLENGE TO AMERICAN LIFE

The Challenge to American Life

EDITED BY
Andrew S. Berky

Essay Index Reprint Series

 BOOKS FOR LIBRARIES PRESS
FREEPORT, NEW YORK

College Library, Wayne, Nebr.

Copyright © 1956 by Schwenkfelder Library

Reprinted 1971 by arrangement with
G. P. Putnam's Sons

INTERNATIONAL STANDARD BOOK NUMBER:
0-8369-2143-7

LIBRARY OF CONGRESS CATALOG CARD NUMBER:
76-134052

PRINTED IN THE UNITED STATES OF AMERICA

CONTENTS

FOREWORD 7
Andrew S. Berky

SCIENCE AND INDUSTRY 17
Gaylord P. Harnwell, *president of the University of Pennsylvania*

SPIRITUAL MAN 39
Ralph Cooper Hutchison, *president of Lafayette College*

THE DEMOCRATIC PROCESS 57
James MacGregor Burns, *Williams College*

INDIVIDUAL FREEDOM 81
Henry Steele Commager, *Columbia University*

WORLD PEACE 105
Joseph E. Johnson, *president of the Carnegie Endowment for International Peace*

FOREWORD

Nations, even as individuals, have a remorseless tendency to bobble along on the sea of life, quite unmindful of the absence of a planned itinerary or, for that matter, without any conscious destination in mind. To be sure, the sea has been running rough in recent years and any apparent lack of navigation may be ascribed to a total preoccupation with merely remaining afloat. But, as Ralph Waldo Emerson once observed, "the most advanced nations are always those who navigate the most," and excellence in navigation demands that position and course be determined at frequent intervals, preoccupations notwithstanding.

There is some reason to believe that much of the danger to America stems from indecision, confused and misguided thinking—or downright bewilderment. This is largely so because Americans today are faced with a staggering array of problems and challenges. There are any number of expedient solutions and responses, but there is a growing suspicion that in some areas of endeavor the nation no longer functions in the traditional American pattern. If this is so, would it be

FOREWORD

advisable to get back on course, or do circumstances justify continued exploration of other itineraries? In short, where do we go from here?

Any thoughtful consideration of this question would of necessity involve a re-evaluation of American ideals and goals, along with a brief study of the basic problems. This was the general approach suggested to each of the distinguished contributors to this study. They were invited to present their views in lecture form at the Schwenkfelder Library, Pennsburg, Pennsylvania, which institution originally conceived and sponsored the project.

The expositions were aimed at the proverbial man-on-the-street, that hypothetical individual who plays the all-important role in developing American civilization by virtue of his selections, attitudes, reactions, and opinions. The sum total of his past responses has produced the America we know today and he is currently hard at work forging our future days. If he is given a fair opportunity to understand the problems and challenges, there is no reason to believe that his deportment will be anything less than courageous and commonsensical.

The main task then is to keep whittling away at the multitude of secondary complexities until the basic issues are exposed and resolved. The competition for men's minds is keen, if not overwhelming, and the

FOREWORD

average citizen is constantly in need of guidance and direction.

What follows on these pages, then, is a kind of intellectual navigation drawing upon the broad knowledge and sound judgment of some of America's best minds.

ANDREW S. BERKY

THE CHALLENGE TO AMERICAN LIFE

Science and Industry

In the introduction to his thoughtful essay *Modern Science and Modern Man,* James B. Conant says that he was tempted to call the essay: "science and the predicament of the intelligent citizen." The disquietude and apprehension is, of course, a direct result of the development of the atomic bomb, a superb accomplishment by any yardstick. However, unlike a few other spectacular productions, such as nylon and the aptly labeled "wonder" drugs, the implications surrounding our ability to destroy matter are rather enormous and the centuries-old carefree camaraderie that existed between layman and scientist has been re-opened for negotiation in some quarters.

Happily, there is every reason to believe that the necessary adjustments are being made and the mid-century American will learn to live with his new concepts, meeting the challenges posed by science and industry with characteristic vigor and imagination. In no other area of performance have our efforts been crowned with more success and each door that is opened into the unknown reveals a larger door beyond.

SCIENCE AND INDUSTRY

The layman has probably always approached the scientist with a sense of awe and admiration. We may smile at the shortcomings and failure of medieval alchemists, but certainly their contemporaries did not. And if we are still inclined to laugh at their dream of transmuting baser metals into gold, how shall we then receive the recent news that it took seven industrial scientists four years and thousands of attempts to produce man-made diamonds identical with those of nature? The man of science is more than ever the explorer and adventurer, "the spiritual descendent of Marco Polo and Magellan and Captain Cook, pushing out across a wide frontier beyond which lies a territory as full of surprise as the western oceans ever were."

Such a man is Gaylord P. Harnwell, widely recognized as one of the most able scientists in this country. A native of Evanston, Illinois, he received his education at Haverford College, Cambridge University, England, and Princeton. Prior to becoming chairman of the department of physics at the University of Pennsylvania in 1938, Dr. Harnwell was a fellow of the National Research Council at the California Institute of Technology and a Professor of Physics at Princeton University. Editor of, and contributor to, many scientific journals, he was also the author of *Experimental Atomic Physics* in 1936, and *Principles of Electricity and Electromagnetism* in 1939. During World War II,

14

Dr. Harnwell was the director of the United States Navy war research laboratories at the University of California. In 1953 Gaylord Harnwell was elected to the presidency of the University of Pennsylvania.

SCIENCE AND INDUSTRY

by Gaylord P. Harnwell

THAT the words "Science" and "Industry" should be linked together as representing a most significant area in the challenges faced by our nation today is in itself of great significance and would have been a source of great surprise to preceding generations. Our times are unique in history, and it is a matter of no small moment that we should talk about science and industry as two aspects of human endeavor which are intimately linked. Perhaps it is in order that we review briefly the growth of science and its technology and also the much longer story of industry throughout the ages, and then survey some of the unique problems with which we are confronted in these areas of interest today.

Industry, in its elemental form, is as old as the human race. Specialization has been a hallmark of social development from the days when seeds were first planted and cultivated and animals were kept in herds and byres. Industrial specialization, however, was severely limited in prehistoric times and extended little beyond the family unit except for persons skilled in the chipping of flint or the practice of priestly and healing arts. From the dawn of history until the industrial revolution, the development of industry has been slow and somewhat sporadic in nature, contributed to by random discovery and inventions.

Individual achievements and the skills of local groups have frequently been lost by wars or social upheavals, until the phrase "lost arts" has become a common one in the area of skills and crafts. It is not that the achievements of our forefathers in this area have been neglected, but they have represented the genius of individuals or small groups denied broad access to current cultural knowledge, limited in their facilities and markets, and subject to the constant hazards of a predatory and unstable society.

Agriculture and animal husbandry were among the first of the industries to develop, but progress in these pursuits caused little comment in the course of history. Housing and food processing were domestic, family arts, and they have achieved the status of industries only within recent times. The use of skins and fabrics was dependent upon domestic animals and a few suitable plants, and their fabrication into clothing and other furnishings was possibly the oldest of the guild activities and is associated with the early rise of European commerce and industry.

The general area of industry relating to weapons

SCIENCE AND INDUSTRY

and tools again extends back to the most distant antiquity, and indeed the archaeologist records his eras in terms of materials such as stone, bronze, and iron, the working of which was currently mastered by our forefathers in successive stages of their history. Skill in the making of glass and pottery was encountered in many localities both before the dawn of history and as the great classical empires developed. As in the case of tools and weapons, pottery and its decorative patterns provide a principal means for the study of ancient civilizations. The potter's skill was a distinctive local attribute, and the shards found in ancient sites tell not only of the development of this industry but of the spread of its products by commerce three or four thousand years ago.

Such arts as those which we have mentioned characterized the growth of civilization, and as we look back upon their development we are impressed not only by the individual genius of our forebears but by the limitations constantly surrounding them which prevented the broad expansion of the crafts which they evolved. Their abilities were limited by the forces at their disposal. Manpower and animal power were supplemented by the power of wind and water but rarely until comparatively recent times.

This fascinating facet in the development of our world has little contact with the development of science

Gaylord P. Harnwell

as this is commonly conceived. Though the Babylonians and Egyptians became expert in counting and measurement, the Greeks are generally credited with the initiation of science as an intellectual activity. In distinction to the authoritarian and priestly traditions of the early empires, the Greek ethos was one of freedom and individual initiative. Speculation was encouraged and intellectual abilities were stimulated. Freedom from prejudice and fear which had dawned in the Aegean 2500 years ago provided an atmosphere in which the intellect of man could expand and inquire and seek to improve his understanding of the world and of his fellow men.

The people who participated in this civilization from the level of free speculative men were not those concerned with industry. The arts and skills, and particularly the chores, were the lot more frequently of slaves, and industry and science were poles apart in the golden age of Greece. Nor did they find common ground in the succeeding eras of the rise of Rome or the civilizations of the Middle or Far East. In the Renaissance, artists studied the properties of materials and achieved great skill in their employment. They were practical men and contributed greatly to the fundamentals of current crafts, but again the limitations imposed by the isolation of communities and the limited strength of men and beasts prevented the juncture of science and industry. The two remained separate all through the eighteenth century, the relative growth of science being much more rapid than that of industry. The juncture between these two areas of human interest came about primarily as a result of the achievements of scientists of the past century.

The reduction of the steam engine to a practical device by Savery, Newcomen, and Watt and the invention of the electrical motor by Faraday marked the advent of the era which we now find in full flower in America. As we look back over the centuries we realize that our present society has undergone revolutionary changes within the past half dozen generations, and that these changes can be attributed primarily to three great forces in our society—the rise of education, the development of power sources, and the advancement of industrial techniques in communication and transportation. The brief period of history which has been marked by the fruitful union of science and industry is coincident with that in which our country has matured as a nation and has accepted the responsibility of leadership throughout the world.

What can be said about these factors which have been most influential in bringing about the world in which we live today? Education is a broad word which includes both teaching and research. Elementary education has brought to the attention of our youth the

Gaylord P. Harnwell

stimulating achievements of the past and has provided a society of free and equal men capable of participating in the development of their society. Books have preserved the results of man's efforts in the past, and research has advanced our control over our environment in all fields of endeavor. Though wars are still with us, we have domestic tranquillity in which the arts and industries can flourish unhindered by the predatory depredations of the local anti-social elements which marked the growth of Western civilization from the Middle Ages until the rise of strong governmental units. Education is indeed the most important factor in the growth of civilization and in the formation of the character of our country.

However, the availability of flexible power sources is a factor which is frequently under-emphasized, and without it life would be very different for us all. The Industrial Revolution, with its "dark satanic mills," was an unlovely interlude in the early days of steam, but now we can see that our well-being would be impossible without the steam engine, the electric motor, the internal combustion engine, and even the jet airplane. A few skilled people can now do the work of many. The bonds of drudgery which depressed large segments of the population have been loosened, hours of work have been shortened, conditions of life have

SCIENCE AND INDUSTRY

been ameliorated, leisure has been achieved, and great comfort has come to everyone.

Without the benefits of communication and mechanical transportation, however, we would be a series of small island societies, unintegrated and extending over vast areas of the cultivable surface of the earth. Great nations such as ours can only operate and promote their industry and their commerce as an integrated unit through the medium of rapid communication and expeditious travel. In terms of science, the development of power, the perfection of electrical communication, the application of energy sources to transportation, the development of the arts of metallurgy and ceramics, and the introduction of automatic surveillance and control have all stemmed from physics and its associated engineering disciplines.

Closely related development by the science of chemistry in fuels, rubbers, textiles, dyes, coatings, drugs, and so forth, have provided the materials characterizing our present surroundings. Biology, too, has contributed in the control of agriculture and animal husbandry, the development of medicine, and the control of bacteria, viruses, etc., through antibiotic agents. The physical and biological sciences represent the areas of educational activity which have most obviously and demonstrably contributed to the unique character which American life has taken on in our generation.

Gaylord P. Harnwell

Life is longer, more healthy, and lived in greater comfort. Each individual is more effective through the tools and facilities which science and industry have devised. As a people we are freer from toil than many preceding generations, and we enjoy leisure for the employment of our interests and talents which would have been the envy of the greatest men and women in any preceding generation.

The interaction of science, technology, and industry in our present-day society presents many points of interest which illuminate both the importance of the interaction for our welfare and the factors which make it effective. The fruits of science and technology assist industry in the improvement of its processes and its products, many times leading to completely new industries and products so transformed and diversified as to lose all generic relationship with the earlier fruits of man's industry. In turn, the products of industry in the form of improved materials, instruments, and devices place facilities in the hands of scientists and technologists, which enable them to conduct their exploratory experiments more effectively, and in turn contribute more significantly to further industrial progress.

Though the electrical industry would not exist had it not been for Faraday and Maxwell and their successors in physics and electrical engineering, it would

SCIENCE AND INDUSTRY

likewise not exist in the form we know it were it not for the development of refined metallurgical processes, the evolution of reliable dielectrics, and all of the special skills which have gone into the electronic arts. In turn, the electrical industry provides us with convenient and efficient power, permits instantaneous communication, and contributes to the transportation facilities which enable us to cross the continent in the fraction of a day. When science and industry existed separately in nascent form in our society, they were relatively small factors in the daily lives of individuals. Now their combined results permeate the structure of society and influence the daily lives of us all.

The rate of growth of science and industry is roughly proportional to the success which these activities have had in producing a situation in terms of knowledge and facilities which stimulates further progress. Thus the growth is exponential, and the optimistic forecasts of the further amenities to human existence which can be anticipated are probably more conservative than our experience would justify. Currently, such great industries as petroleum, power, communication, and others estimate that their operations double in every decade that passes. This is a tremendous rate of growth without parallel in any previous period in history, and it poses many problems for the future. The growth of science is less easily measured, and probably no quanti-

Gaylord P. Harnwell

tative assessment has meaning beyond a narrow segment of the future. Our educational system is subject to great strain at the moment, and we can foresee problems of greater magnitude in the future. Most of these are concerned with the availability of scientists and technologists in the future.

Though the understanding of science is less complete on the part of our citizenry than we could wish, there is little question but that in practice our modern technology is in the forefront of the minds of all of us, whether we be students or adults. At one time the arts and the sciences were distinguished antithetically in our college curricula, but in a very real sense the sciences have come to be a leading art and one probably most characteristic of twentieth century society. Technology plays the more sparkling and colorful role in the things about us, but the methods of science are slowly but surely having as far-reaching effect upon our methods of thought that contribute to objective and dispassionate analysis and synthesis of the factors affecting all human situations.

The enormous change in our daily lives brought about through the scientific and industrial revolution of the past half century brings with it problems which are of the greatest concern to us in the future. The fact that each person in the United States has *100 horse power* rather than *1 man power* at his disposal exerts

SCIENCE AND INDUSTRY

a pressure upon patterns of life and social customs which must result in enormous if unpredictable changes. The lengthening of life, the improvement in health, the greater ease with which our necessary functions can be performed, and the resultant leisure enjoyed by everyone must result in a society very different from that which our forefathers have known. At present we are passing through a stage in which the strains of growth and change threaten to exert intolerable pressures upon the social trends which we observe.

As an instance of the conflicts which we can see before us, one may consider the demands for the services of scientific personnel and the apparent inability of our educational system to supply appropriately trained and motivated men and women. In the Sunday issue of *The New York Times* one sees advertisements for electronic engineers, engineers and physicists, nuclear development managers, gas turbine engineers, and a host of other highly trained and specialized persons upon whom the development program of technical industry must depend. Such persons are not now available in numbers which meet the demand of industry, and the rate at which they are being trained is still less commensurate with the needs which we anticipate for the future. A recent survey, for instance, of the study of physics in high schools shows that during the past half century the national percentage enroll-

Gaylord P. Harnwell

ment in physics courses has dropped by a factor of nearly six. During this interval there has been little change in the percentage enrollment in chemistry, and though a considerable enrollment increase has been observed in biology, this has not kept pace with the needs even in that field.

The rate at which engineers are graduated from our universities and technical institutes has dropped somewhat in recent years to an annual figure approaching 30,000 persons. Our estimated need is for at least twice that rate of availability, and what figures are available indicate that in the Soviet Union engineers are being trained at approximately twice the rate they are in the United States. Thus it is clear that a brake will be placed upon our rate of technical advance unless these trends are averted in the future.

The causes of this situation are doubtless multiple and imperfectly understood. Some appear, however, to be reasonably obvious, such as the greater financial rewards available in commerce and trade and the greater prestige rewards among publicists, entertainers, and in other areas of endeavor. Contrasting this situation with the Soviet Union, for example, I quote from Mr. Ashby in *The New York Times:*

> When he comes to make his choice, the Moscow boy is influenced by the immense prestige, delib-

SCIENCE AND INDUSTRY

erately built up by the state, of engineering and science. Newspaper headlines there go to the scientist, not to the film stars or the football players or thugs. Every expedition to discover minerals, every new meteorological station in the Arctic, every improvement in making aluminum alloys, is written up for the newspapers in the racy style of a sports review.

More than all this, the books written for children ...are used to boost the status of scientists. The heroes of schoolboy stories are not spies or detectives but engineers or scientists. To measure the salinity of water so as to irrigate the deserts of Dagestan, to hunt for uranium in the forests of Yakutski—these are the adventures which fill the story books. Even medicine is sissy by comparison with engineering and is becoming more and more regarded as a job for sister to do.

Particularly basic in the problems facing us in the training of scientists and technologists is the difficulty in establishing the courses through which such persons receive their education. The teacher is an essential cog in the machine which provides an educated citizenry, and we have been particularly remiss in permitting the teaching profession to suffer both financially and in prestige in present-day society. Like the

Gaylord P. Harnwell

ministry, it is an honorable but poorly rewarded calling, and we should not be surprised if our basic abilities to take advantage of the gifts of science and industry are severely handicapped by the weakness developing in our educational system.

The disparity between the needs for specialized education and the number of persons embarking upon such careers is but one of the many areas of strain which we can see developing under the influence of the new wine of technical life being poured into the old customs and habits of our society. A second is brought about by the role of science in World War II and the development of weapons which in the hands of small irresponsible bodies of men can become a serious threat to the great nations of the world. Again a serious concern is felt by many that human responsibility and conscience is falling rapidly behind in comparison with human abilities and physical accomplishments, with the result that the balance of our life is shifted from the older and more familiar ways through which our race has passed. The long struggle through recorded history between the liberal and authoritarian traditions which has marked the political development of the Western Hemisphere has proceeded without catastrophe or cataclysm because of the relative impotence of groups of differing ideologies. Given the changing circumstances of today, however, we must be

SCIENCE AND INDUSTRY

concerned lest our wisdom prove inadequate to control the forces which we have brought into being.

We have seen the natural sciences usher in the nuclear age and with it new problems peculiar to the growing interaction between society and technology. The past decade has been one of alternating tension and near despair as we have attempted to accommodate this new power in our midst. Certain positive signs have appeared recently, however, in the conduct of human affairs which augur well for the rational control of these great physical forces. Our President has called for a new approach to the atom centered around the application of nuclear science in promoting world peace, and our Congress has responded with appropriate legislation.

Since these developments it has been gratifying to observe the quickened interest on the part of American industries concerned with nuclear applications to such fields as electric power, chemical, metallurgical and food processes, and propulsion. Of course, the beneficent use of atomic energy has been seen in the field of medicine for some time, and progress in this area has been keenly followed by scientist and lay person alike.

In our relations with other countries hopeful signs are likewise emerging, as our nation gives positive expression to its desire to share scientific knowledge

Gaylord P. Harnwell

and methods with all peoples, and especially with those who are the victims of poverty, disease, and ignorance. Technological personnel from outside the United States are presently here, at our government's invitation, to study nuclear developments at one of the national laboratories. Of much significance too was the United Nations Conference on the Peaceful Uses of Nuclear Energy, which convened in Geneva in August of 1955. This marked the first time since the United Nations discussions of 1947-48 that scientists and engineers from both sides of the "Iron Curtain" sat down together in an attempt to arrive at an understanding of questions of a purely technical nature. Their deliberations could well mark the start of a new era of international cooperation.

With or without continued understanding among the nations of the world, however, we in the United States are faced with a great challenge—that of orienting ourselves to the nuclear age and to contemporary developments which are certain to affect every facet of the American way of life.

These and other vast problems are beyond our individual solutions, but to the extent that they are recognized and we set our course in allowance for their perils, we can at least take the most intelligent action we may devise. Education has been largely responsible for the progress of mankind to date, and it may well be the most effective instrument in coping with the problems of the future. The habits of critical and rational thought which the sciences have brought into our curricula cannot but help us in analyzing our needs and in devising means for meeting them.

Again, the religious and ethical criteria which have slowly evolved within our society have guided us to the present day and furnish us with the only inspiration we are likely to achieve in the amelioration of the problems of human intercourse and cooperation. We are greatly in want of the wisdom to employ the facilities with which we have been endowed by science and industry, and the story of our success or failure in this enterprise will be the history of succeeding generations.

Spiritual Man

Some historian of the future looking back over the last forty or fifty years of our history undoubtedly will be prompted to remark: "Well, at least they survived!" Then, being an analytical sort of chap, he will set about trying to determine just why we did survive. There will be no easy answers and this historian of the future will blunder into countless blind alleys.

He will note that as a country we have been warred upon, maligned, intrigued against, and ventilated by all sorts of evil breezes. He will find that there were times when we have been foolish, unwise, misguided, mistaken, and perhaps more astonishing than all of these—we have largely been indifferent. And yet, out of this pattern of confusion will emerge a series of triumphs which far transcend anything the world has seen. To all outward appearances we are still healthy, wealthy, and wise.

But what of that intangible and intimate area of human nature which responds to faith? The historian of the future will hardly characterize our age as being one dominated by faith and reason. He may well be

SPIRITUAL MAN

tempted to say that we lived in a climate of opinion dominated by the three "D's"—doubt, disunity and dismay—the doubt which is at the heart of scientific inquiry, the disunity which is manifest in our art and literature, and the dismay which accompanies our efforts to develop new moral standards.

It seems apparent, then, that the avenues for spiritual values we have developed and cherished for several centuries are no longer going on before us as they once did. Our knowledge accumulates and our wisdom decays. Our churches increase in size and number and their influence appears to diminish.

There are many great challenges facing this country and it would be difficult to say which is the greatest of all. Even so, it would be difficult to comprehend a greater challenge than the one that lies before us in the spiritual realm, for what has a man, or nation, profited if he shall gain the whole world and lose his own soul?

Ralph Cooper Hutchison is a native of Colorado and he received his education at Sterling College, Lafayette College, Harvard, Princeton Theological Seminary, and the University of Pennsylvania. A naval aviator in World War I, Dr. Hutchison has continued his interest in aviation by serving as chairman of the Pennsylvania Aero Commission since 1943. Ordained to the ministry of the Presbyterian Church in 1922, he served the church in various departments of Christian Education until 1926 when he became the dean of Alborz College, Teheran, Persia. In 1931, at the age of 33, Dr. Hutchison was elected to the presidency of Washington and Jefferson College, a position he held until 1945 when he became the president of Lafayette College.

SPIRITUAL MAN

by Ralph Cooper Hutchison

AMERICA is unique. There are those who deny this, who insist that it is no more than a young nation temporarily endowed by the resources of an unexploited continent—that in time it will go the way of all nations and empires. These who so claim would be right if the uniqueness of this people did lie in the unexploited and virgin continent on which they established their first colonies. But this is not the distinctive uniqueness which characterizes this people. The truly significant fact about the United States is that it has been populated by wave after wave of fugitives from the tyranny of older governments in Europe and Asia.

From the beginning there were those who came for adventure, those who were motivated by greed, and those who were escaping from something other than tyranny. But the mass of fugitives was leavened by those fine, spiritual, and frequently well-educated people who sought a land where they might be free to worship, and beyond religious and political tyranny. No nation in all history has been so endowed by noble people with basically spiritual ideals. It was not one exodus as in the case of the Israelites, but wave after wave continuing to the present day. This constant and unceasing migration of those who would have freedom from tyranny has poured into this nation an unending stream of strength. This makes America different, gives it something no other nation has had and could result in an historical development which defies all the typical curves of national destinies.

Amongst these fugitives from tyranny there has been an extraordinary diversity of religious beliefs, and even some who sought the freedom to have no particular belief. It is therefore difficult to generalize and define a common spiritual heritage. But it must be attempted because the attack on the spiritual ideals of America is precisely in this area of common ideals, not in that of particular creeds. This is the reason that the attack is dangerous. When a particular creed or theology or belief is attacked, the danger is pinpointed and can be met. But when the vague field of common spiritual idealism is invaded, then no particular group is alerted, no one takes up the defense and the enemy makes progress in the fog and the night. We wake up in the morning to find all of our sectors surrounded and our camps infiltrated.

Of these common convictions of the spiritual idealism of the varied fugitives from tyranny, the first to be named was the belief in an overruling God, creator of

SPIRITUAL MAN

the Universe, a person in the n'th degree and in the ultimate sense. Among His many attributes there was one of greatest significance for our discussion here. From God there emanated a higher law of right and wrong. This law was called "higher" because it bore no relationship to the legal codifications of human governments. It did not depend upon time or place. It did not depend upon the health, needs, or conditions of the individual man. It did not vary with men of high or those of low estate, or change with the seasons. Man could never fully comprehend that higher law but spiritual men made an unending effort to do so. They sought for it in divine revelation, in the lessons of history, in their inner consciousness, and in the discoveries of the natural world. Though hard to discover, all knowledge thereof fragmentary, and obscured by the very limitations of the human mind, still there was no question that the ordinances and laws of God were there. Understanding of and obedience to that law was obviously the way, not only to happiness, but the way of life. Defiance of that law, either knowingly or unknowingly, was the way of defeat, misery, and death. In brief there was a right and a wrong and in that conviction all of the spiritual sons of America were agreed —Jews, Catholics, Protestants, Calvinists, Armenians, Unitarians, Primitives, Quietists, and transcendentalists. Assailed, attacked, undermined, discredited by its opponents, this is still the conviction of the people of America, and the rich and common heritage which we have from those who came for religious and political freedom.

Second of the great convictions of spiritual America is that concerning the significance of the individual person. Out of this basic conviction came the movement for freedom from political tyranny. Its roots are in Christianity and in Christ who came to seek and to save that which was lost, who gave His Life that "whosoever" believeth in Him should not perish but have eternal life, who wept over the city of Jerusalem but called men one by one. This common creed is that Christ came not to save the empire but the men in the empire who were then to turn their regenerated powers to the salvation of society and empire. This common creed is that each man lives alone and dies alone, each has his own destiny, each chooses the way he will go, each should be free within reason to achieve his own highest intellectual and spiritual fulfillment. The whole structure of democratic government has as its primary function the protection of the individual in those rights. The only sound hope for the social order rests on the fulfillment of the individual obligations which follow upon the exercise of those rights. Challenged by the so-called liberals of government and of religion, repudiated by the most tyrannical and brutal despotisms abroad, this has always been and still is part of the common creed of the spiritual sons of America.

Third, our common spiritual conviction is that these laws of God, these rights of man, these responsibilities of the individual to the social order should be preached and taught, but not otherwise forced upon the minds and consciences of the human race. To "go ye into all the world and teach all nations" was the last command of the Master. To force men into the way of righteousness by police powers, to legislate them into social progress by laws, to brain wash them from their evil ways, to torture men to the confessional, to hypnotize the social order with mass psychiatry, to terrorize them into discipline, was never in the creed of spiritual America. This therefore became a teaching and a preaching land. Education by conviction has been our ideal. Occasional aberrations in our history, from this teaching, persuading mission are exceptions which only point up the rule, the faith, the belief of our people that this is the way of social reform, this is the way of peace, this is the way of salvation. This is, we believe humbly and sincerely, the way of God.

Probably other common spiritual ideals and convictions could be defined but these three are the ones that are under attack in our day and therefore deserve special attention in this discussion. Because they are common to most all of us, they are the ideals which must be attacked. Because they are common, they are least defended.

The attack on these ideals is world wide. We recognize it in its extreme forms abroad but do not recognize it at home, because it takes on the form of an angel. The philosophers agree in calling this opponent Scientific Humanism. There may be as many as thirty different combinations of teachings, each one of which has equal right to this term. We therefore are free to choose our own just so we are certain that the teachings chosen are properly and honestly in this area. And let it be said that there are many teachings of Scientific Humanism which are true, which constitute fine correctives for our thinking, and which if accepted will purify and elevate our Christian program. But here are those which constitute a particular danger.

First, there is no supernatural. All is natural and all truth is subject to discovery and determination through science. Science, dealing with that which can be proven to the senses, is indeed the way of life and the only way of life. The convictions based on the supernatural, upon fancied revelation, upon faith in the unseen and the unknown are an outworn relic of the past, fetishes which, as such philosophers say, no intelligent man can accept today. As a consequence, there is no higher law, no law written in the heart, no law on the tablets of stones, no law revealed in the sublimities of nature, no law in the inner conscience, no law of God. The only ethic is that objectively legislated by the state, or revealed conclusively in the natural world through science.

Second, following the lead of Bacon, Lenin, Hobgen, and Bernal, there are no values save material and scientific realities. This is thorough-going rationalism. Truth is only that which produces bread for the needy, prosperity for society. The ultimate measure of value or rightness is the result. The end therefore not only justifies the means, it is the only justification of the means. If an act or an attitude or a procedure produces food, profit, or power for society it is good. If it does not produce materialistic and observable results which are desirable, it is evil. Christ on the Cross was not good regardless of his inherent attitude or purposes because he did not bring food for the poor, or prosperity to Palestine. No material results, hence evil.

Third, the objective of all life is social progress. Here is one of the greatest values and greatest vices of scientific humanism, because social progress is good. The scientific humanist has arbitrarily inherited and adopted the concept from the Christian ethic. But he makes it the supreme good and only goal. Therefore the good of the many is the final criterion. The individual is nothing. The minority is nothing. Unless it is controlling, the majority is nothing. If they conflict with the despot's concept of social good the rights of the individual do not exist. Nor need he himself exist. Individuals of the highest intrinsic value may be brain washed or pillaged or liquidated if it is for "social progress." Minorities may be exterminated if it is for "social progress." Social progress is the only norm, the only ideal, the only objective. All other values are dismissed.

Finally, since the end justifies the means, because social progress is the only value, and since the individual is of no significance, the most brutal and unbridled force is justified. All the developing power of science is to be used to bring about the social progress desired. Hence the use of laws to achieve social progress, the use of the police state, of war, of terror, of torture, of psychiatry, is justified and in fact inevitable in order to achieve social progress in the shortest time possible. The scientific humanists even go one step further. They anticipate that through the use of genetics and selective breeding they will be able not only to achieve the transmutation of the species, but to predetermine the type of man to be produced and to acquire control of the thinking and temperament of the generations of the future, thus forcing with ultimate power the social progress which is their present objective.

SPIRITUAL MAN

These elements of scientific humanism are direct attacks on the several great common spiritual principles which were outlined in the beginning of this discussion. Here the battle line is drawn. Here we take up arms and fight—or should do so. The fact is that we are not doing it. We have been infiltrated. We have been deceived. We are going along with these evils.

Inflamed by the fad for social progress and reform, we have given up the teaching of social idealism and have embarked on what we call a liberal movement. We are achieving social progress by legislation. Instead of persuading men we command them. We tried it with the Blue Laws. We tried it with the Prohibition Amendment. We are trying it now in the matter of racial relations by forcing desegregation on the South and by the FEPC laws in the North. The New Deal was characterized by law after law intended to achieve the reforms which should be achieved by the persuasion, education, and evangelization of free men. We are being taken into camp by the enemy whose creedal purpose is the use of force to secure social progress.

In our moral judgments we have gone over into the enemies' territory because while not denying God it is becoming very common to deny any higher law. We have insisted in our teachings and in our preachings that all laws are relative to the individual, to his situation, to his wishes, and his purposes. We have substituted an opportunistic and relative ethic for the absolute. We are becoming a compromising, relativistic, uncertain people recognizing no absolute right or wrong, no higher law.

In our political and religious liberalism we have been tempted as Christ was on the mountain to think only of the social group and no longer of the individual. We have been beguiled by the idea that if we can save society, each individual will be caught up in some kind of corporate salvation. We lose the evangelical passion which reaches out for each individual and are bent on the larger group, the good of the many, disregarding the significance as well as the rights of the individual.

Finally, in government and probably in business we believe that the end justifies the means. At the moment, for the laudable purpose of peace, we are willing to compromise with tyranny. More and more our people seem to favor the recognition of the brutal and bloody despotism of China, the disregard of unjust war being waged in Korea and Indonesia, the imprisonment of our flyers and our citizens, the violations of the armistice—if such compromises with evil, slavery, and tyranny will bring the highly desirable objective of peace. Never have we been so tempted to compromise, to use evil means in order to attain some desired social good.

SPIRITUAL MAN

Many believe that there has been a moral breakdown in our social order. Dishonesty in business, corruption, bribery, marital and sexual immorality, corruption in government—all of these, insofar as they do exist to any great extent, are the reflection of a philosophy which has no absolutes in right and wrong and which believes compromise involving violations is right under certain circumstances.

Most striking of the results of scientific humanism has been the phenomenon of well-educated people of good inclinations who have fallen victim to the propaganda of Communism. Alger Hiss and Judith Coplan are illustrations. The mystery of their actions is explained by the scientific humanism to which they were undoubtedly exposed during their educational careers. They were not taught Communism in school and college but they were taught passionately that social progress is the supreme good and goal of society, that such an end justifies any means, that force therefore is justifiable and desirable in attaining this end, that nothing is wrong in itself and that there is no higher ethic or law. So taught, they had the formula. When they did come in contact with Communism they were "sitting ducks" for its more radical proposals. Here, as both have said, was a program for social progress of mankind which they wanted to help. The liquidation of millions in its brutal cause they could overlook because the individual was nothing, society everything. The betrayal of their trusts and treason to their nation was not inherently wrong in the first place because nothing in itself was wrong. Therefore they were justified in accepting the Communist program, overlooking its world-wide terror and massacre, and betraying their own nation and people to help that program of so-called "social progress." Without Communist teachers or professors, there are possibly millions being inculcated with the gentle philosophy of scientific humanism, millions who can later be victims of the extremes of this same teaching which is ruthless, marching, terrorizing, Communism, dripping with the blood of humanity and bent upon the conquest of the world.

The only basic remedy is in the aggressive and convinced teachings of Christianity in church, home, and school, in the streets and the byways, and throughout the nations of the world. That teaching is that individual man is the supreme value in life and that each one has therefore ineradicable dignity and an eternal destiny, that his rights cannot be taken away even for the good of the many, even for social progress.

This remedial teaching is that the first purpose of life is the development and salvation of the individual, who will in turn redeem society.

This teaching is that there is a higher law of right

and wrong, that it is the law of God and that God is real, imminent, conscious, intelligent, concerned, involved and that His ordinances and statutes are absolute, eternal, and applicable.

This teaching is therefore that some things are wrong no matter if the end is good; that the massacre of millions, the enslavement of man, the twisting and torturing of the human mind is wrong even if the objective is social progress.

Finally, this teaching is that persuasion and teaching should be used in the redemption of society, not force. This is the way of God, who has all power but who obviously withholds the use of that power leaving man free. John pictures God in these words, "Behold, I stand at the door and knock. If any man will hear my voice, and open the door, I will come in to him and will sup with him and he with me." God will not batter down the doors with the butt of a bayonet, nor rush into the house with an armed force, nor compel goodness with legislation. It means rather that he will attempt only to persuade, to teach, to convince. He only knocks at the door, and waits.

In this age of power we are more tempted than ever before to use force for the achievement of the ends which we think are good. We are intrigued that we have far more power over mankind, over the mind of man, than ever before. Not only in government and in international affairs but in the church itself we are forming councils and taking measures to exert power in Washington or in the state, or community. Men of good will advocating reform are intoxicated with new powers and utterly deceived by the subtle words of scientific humanism and false liberalism tempting them to use that power to set up the Kingdom of God.

How then may we hope to return in strength to the spiritual ideals on which this nation was founded? Must all of the people of this nation be reached with the truth of God and warned of this false philosophy? No, it is only necessary that a hard core of society understand. The trouble is not that the false philosophies discussed here have penetrated society but that they have invaded the church of Christ itself, and corrupted its preachings and teachings. The preservation of the spiritual idealism of America does not demand a universal conviction on these matters but just in the core, that is, in the church. The essential thing now is that the church of Christ purge its own thinking, return to unqualified faith in the ordinances of God, in the divinity of the individual, and in the use of persuasions as the only method for the establishment of the Kingdom of God.

The Democratic Process

In recent days, few areas of government function have received as much attention as the burdens of the Presidency. This is hardly a new development for Americans have always placed heavy demands upon the person they have elevated to democracy's highest position. Abraham Lincoln rarely complained about his exhausting duties, but it was inevitable that he should feel constrained to pass comment: "I sometimes fancy," he once remarked, "that every one of the numerous grist ground through here daily, from a Senator seeking a war with France down to a poor woman after a place in the Treasury Department, darted at me with thumb and finger, plucked out their special piece of vitality and carried it off."

Suffice it to say that government office has worn out a long series of good and gifted men. But what of the government itself, this vague and vast piece of machinery that exercizes direct control over 160 million people and indirect control over many more? Is it not possible that this machine too can become weary and haggard? The constitution has been amended, repaired, and reinterpreted, and yet it is substantially no different than that priceless contract accepted by Americans over 150 years ago. At the time, one English observer, perhaps with good reason, observed that our frame of government was little more than "nonsense on stilts." His logic may have been incontestable, but he overlooked the fact that if you can become acclimated to the height, you can always see further.

John Knox Jessup recently observed that America's "greatest manufacturing achievement was the manufacture of the Constitution ... and great artists of politics have kept it in repair ever since." If we can accept the thought that this superb piece of machinery is still serviceable, vigorous, and equal to the tasks placed before it, our chief concern should then be: what are we doing with this frame of government that has been handed down to us? We can build a superb house, but it will be no better than the living that goes on inside of it. We can construct a magnificent automobile, but if it serves no more purpose than cutting down the time on the speed run to the local drug store, it might better not have been built. Similarly, in time of war, the most technically advanced airplane is little more than a platform for getting guns closer to the enemy and, of course, the world's best form of government will come to grief if it is not properly prescribed, administered, and accepted.

THE DEMOCRATIC PROCESS

By and large, Americans have worked pretty hard at this business of government and there are times, April 15 being one, when we wished rather wistfully, that we'd taken things a bit easy. Apart from financial relationships, all of us in recent years have felt more keenly perhaps than ever before, that our relationship with the government has persistently become more intimate. We have come to realize that there have been decided changes in concept and administration, that new programs have been launched which are irrevocable. These things are the result of government at work, the democratic process, if you will.

Most of us are alike in that we spend all too little time in actually thinking about government policy and activity. It's much simpler to react to something that somebody else "thunk" up. If the problem is too complex, we react by avoiding it or by getting mad. Both devices are socially acceptable, but in the long run there's no substitute for the hardest kind of thinking.

James MacGregor Burns is a native of Melrose, Massachusetts, a graduate of Williams College, with a doctorate from Harvard University. He served with the United States infantry G-2 Division in the invasions of Saipan, Guam, and Okinawa, for which service he was awarded the Bronze Star Medal.

Prior to his army service, Dr. Burns served as Executive Secretary of the National War Labor Board's Nonferrous Metals Division. He continued his government work in the War Department in 1946, served as a consultant to the Hoover Commission in 1949 and also as a consultant to the Little Hoover Commission in 1950. Dr. Burns continued his studies at the London School of Economics in 1949, he was a faculty member of the Salzburg Seminar in American Studies at Salzburg, Austria in 1954 and is currently a fellow of the Social Science Research Council. Dr. Burns is the author of the following books: *Congress on Trial, Government By the People,* and *Roosevelt: The Lion and the Fox.* He is a frequent contributor to *The New York Times Sunday Magazine.* Through all of this he has somehow managed to continue a relationship with Williams College as Professor of Political Science.

THE DEMOCRATIC PROCESS

by James MacGregor Burns

THERE is a saying about Americans so old, so hoary, so over-quoted that I would not mention it except that it points up so well the dilemma facing anyone taking a fresh look at the democratic process as part of a re-evaluation of American ideals and goals. That hoary old saying is that "God takes special care of drunkards, children, and the United States of America." It is an over-used saying mainly because it seeks to speak the truth. God *does* seem to reserve a special benignity for Americans. But if he does, it raises the whole dilemma of whether we need to re-evaluate the democratic process, whether we need to reconsider the governmental system under which we have, materially at least, flourished so well.

Consider our special dispensations—or, if you will, our great good luck. Not only have we inherited this great country with its fabulous natural resources. We have also been the depository of peoples from many other parts of the world, people bringing with them an abundance of talent and energy. We have been blessed with geographical isolation in an epoch when mere geographical position may determine whether or not a nation survives. For none of these fortunate matters —or for others that I could mention—can we take credit as a people; indeed, as in the case of our immigration laws, sometimes we seem to fight against our good fortune.

Or consider the lucky turns of fate that have helped us through history. Our diplomacy during the nineteenth century was often incredibly bad, and our military strength was feeble, but we had the protection of Her Majesty's Fleet in the event that some of our bellicose acts got us into international difficulties. Late in the century we faced mounting unrest and protest from debt-ridden farmers; the problem was solved not through governmental action but largely through greater international supplies of gold. The first decade of this century was marked by a tremendous upsurge of moral feeling against social and economic conditions of the time, especially on the part of middle class people; by the sheerest chance there was projected into the White House a young man named Theodore Roosevelt who was able in brilliant fashion both to respond to, and to temper, the excitement stirred up by the muckrakers. In the 1930's we faced a staggering depression; the problem was solved not by the government but by the coming of war, which required gigantic federal spending and put men and women to work again.

And today our good luck seems to continue. The international situation is critical enough to call for what seems to be the right balance between governmental and private spending—but not critical enough to involve the horrors of total war. Or, in a different area, President and Congress seem unable to deal with the whole problem of civil and social rights—but along comes the most conservative branch of the national government, namely the Supreme Court, and exerts the kind of leadership in this delicate area that we so badly need. Truly this is a nation on which all blessings seem to fall.

Now, in the light of all this, I suppose that we could stop worrying about our problems and go off, all of us, to our separate interests and pleasures, secure in the knowledge that we have this divine protection. Yet I doubt that any of us are so minded. The very fact that we are engaged in re-evaluating the democratic process attests to our belief that the exigencies of our time call at least for some consideration of the need to change our methods, ideals and goals, whether or not we decide they should be changed.

For my own part, I cannot believe that our good fortune will last forever. Perhaps it is in part an instinctive feeling that any nation that smugly assumes the continuation of special or divine dispensation is sure to lose it. But my feeling is based on more than instinct; it is based on what I think is a fairly realistic appreciation of the difficulty, indeed formidability, of the problems sure to arise as we negotiate the hard, rocky, and perilous course through the rest of this century.

What are some of the problems ahead? The first and most serious, of course, is winning a long, tough battle with the Russians for the preservation of the security and independence of the free world—a battle that will continue to spill over into the economic, social, political, and ideological realms. A second is the husbanding of our *human* resources through a comprehensive and continuing effort to extend and to shore up education, health, housing, and other welfare programs. A third is the husbanding of our *natural* resources and the fair and effective development of the great new resource of atomic energy. A fourth is the full sharing of civil, social, and political rights with those who are now denied them. A fifth is the control of our big, booming economy so that it becomes our servant and not our master—so that, for example, abundance is shared with all groups in our society. A sixth is the extension of social and economic welfare to peoples throughout the world—not just because we are competing with the Russians, but because we think that this is good in itself.

Now none of these problems may in itself be more exacting or challenging than those that we have faced in the past. None, for example, may be more difficult or unmanageable than the deepening chasm between North and South that was taking place a century ago. But the difficulties of today are more serious in two respects. In the first place, they are far more complex; they call not just for one key decision or one great effort, but for a series of consistent, carefully timed, soundly conceived, well-coordinated decisions over a long period. Secondly, the problems of today confront us all at one time, and many of them intimately affect one another; for example, there is a close relation between two matters that on first look might seem far apart—namely our civil rights policies at home and our standing with the great uncommitted nations of Asia and Africa. It is safe to say that never has a country faced such a host of different but interrelated problems in such a short span of time. History has caught up with us—and with a vengeance.

Woodrow Wilson was perhaps ahead of his time when, in an earlier era, he expressed certain elements of my point:

James MacGregor Burns

... America is now sauntering through her resources and through the mazes of her politics with easy nonchalance; but presently there will come a time when she will be surprised to find herself grown old,—a country crowded, strained, perplexed, —when she will be obliged to fall back upon her conservatism, obliged to pull herself together, adopt a new regime of life, husband her resources, concentrate her strength, steady her methods, sober her views, restrict her vagaries, trust her best, not her average members.

If, then, I am right in arguing that the multifold challenge to American life calls for a bold re-evaluation of the American democratic process, what kind of re-evaluation is required? As a political scientist I am naturally ready at the drop of a hat to offer a long list of governmental and political reforms. But I do not want to put myself in the position of the dog Epaminondas that William Allen White used to like to tell about. You will recall that Epaminondas was an overly ambitious dog that ate everything in sight, and finally gobbled some plaster of paris off a plasterer's mixing board. After the dog died its master took his remains from around the hardened plaster and wrote on this plaster monument: "Here lies Epaminondas' interior view; he bit off more than he could chew." I do not want to bite off more than I can chew. What I *would* like to do is to offer some guidelines that might be helpful in any bold re-evaluation of our democratic process. Or to change my metaphor, I propose to set up a balance sheet of our major governmental and political institutions with an eye to examining the assets and liabilities of each—all with an eye to a candid reconsideration of the strengths and weaknesses of our democratic process as a whole. Let me emphasize that I am not looking at these institutions in terms of past periods of our history or in the light of abstract sets of conditions, but in terms of the rushing, tumbling stream of problems that face us now and that will probably intensify in the years ahead.

First, our Constitution. I propose two guidelines for a consideration of the Constitution as it embodies or affects the democratic process: that we do not consider it sacred and beyond improvement, but also that we face realistically the fact that changing our constitutional form of government in any major respect is an extremely difficult if not impossible task. Certainly, on the first point, we are a mature enough people not to worship the Constitution blindly. We do not need to agree with an early president of the American Bar Association who proclaimed that the Constitution, like a woman's honor, was not to be "hawked about the country, debated in the newspapers, discussed from the stump, elucidated by pot-house politicians and dung-hill editors." Today we need not look on the Constitution as a closed book, as a magic parchment, as an end in itself. The Constitution, like all elements of government, is but a means to lofty ends as defined by a great people throughout the course of its life history.

But to say this is not to say that we must or can change our constitutional arrangements. On the contrary, our Constitution cannot easily be altered, both because people do not like to see it tampered with and because the formal amending process was carefully set up to prevent its easy modification. President Franklin D. Roosevelt used to like to say: "Give me ten million dollars and I can prevent any amendment, no matter how popular, from going through." And it was no idle boast.

Perhaps I may seem to have boxed myself in, because I appear to be ready to change the Constitution yet I seem doubtful that any real changes can be made. Let me wriggle out of that box right now. What I am implying is that we consider making changes in the *substance* of our Constitution. This indeed is an old American custom, as testified by the development of a strong President and the risk of the party system. Both of these developments—and others I could mention—have profoundly modified the American political system without significantly changing the Constitution. At any rate, any changes in our system that I propose should be understood as involving changes in substance but not changes in the written Constitution.

The second guideline that I propose in any re-evaluation of the American democratic process is that we show a greater confidence in the wisdom—or at least the common sense—of the great mass of the people. Now I know full well that this may sound like a pious mouthing, sound like something that every American hears a hundred times as his teachers talk about the glories of popular self-government or Fourth of July orators preach the wonders of rule by the "peepul." But I mean this in a far more definite and perhaps more extreme sense than one will find in the usual cant about democracy. For the very political preachers and orators who orate about democracy are often the ones who really fear the people when the chips are down. They fear especially the people as gathered in some great mass, as organized in some great national majority, or as concentrated in great, thickly populated urban areas.

Walter Lippmann recently gave candid expression to this kind of fear of the people when he stated, in his important book *The Public Philosophy,* that "public opinion becomes less realistic as the mass to whom information must be conveyed, and argument must be addressed, grows larger and more heterogeneous." Now I would like to take direct exception to this idea. I would argue that the larger the mass of people making the electoral decisions, and above all, the more heterogeneous, the more varied that mass—varied in national origin, in religion, in ideology, in sectional background, in social or economic grouping—the more sensible and forward-looking will be the ensuing decisions.

On what do I base this belief in the collective wisdom of a great and varied collection of people? To some extent on faith—a simple faith in the ultimate wisdom of the people in their collective capacity, provided the issues are put intelligibly and the people are given meaningful choices. To some extent I base this faith in the wisdom of the mass of people on history; we have been the great melting pot, and time and again Americans have made the right general decision when faced with decisive choices. But to a great extent I base my faith in the people on the many indications that in the long run, at least, better decisions can be produced from a group than from the individual. This last notion has been given impressive underpinning in a recent study of political behavior in a fairly typical American city. The social scientists who made the study—Bernard Berelson and his associates—found that any one individual might lack the great qualities that the democratic citizen must possess—for example, any one individual might be uninterested in government or politics, or he might be an extremist in his thinking, or he might be extremely conservative and refuse to consider new ways of doing things, or he might be so radical that he was never content with existing arrangements, or he might be a chronic dissenter, and so on. To look at any one voter made the authors wonder frankly "how a democracy ever solves its political problems." But they came to different conclusions about voters in the mass, because voters collectively seemed to provide a fruitful and dependable balance among all these qualities. In short, balance out in our community one man's qualities of apathy and another man's qualities of excessive concern, one man's conservatism and another man's radicalism, one man's concern with local interest and another man's concern with the national interest—balance these out and we have the makings of a healthy democratic society that can come to sensible decisions.

My third guideline for a re-evaluation of the American democratic process involves the role of Congress. If there is any institution of government that has come under steady and bitter criticism during recent decades, certainly it is our national legislature. This criticism results from many things—from the gerrymandering and other types of unfair districting that distort the representative process, from the tendency of Congressmen to respond unduly to local pressures and sudden waves of emotional public opinion, from the further perverting of the representative process in Congress through such devices as the filibuster in the Senate and the excessive power of the Rules committee in the House. But another and more hidden cause of our dissatisfaction with Congress, I think, is our uncertainty as to just what job we want our national legislature to perform. As we all know, our Founding Fathers originally planned that the Congress as the popular branch, should be the great affirmative law-making power; they planned that the President should be essentially a checking and stabilizing force. In a century and a half or more the President has taken the original place that the Framers of the Constitution planned for Congress. But Congress has not been willing to revert only to the essentially negative role (in the sense of making decisions) that was planned for the Presidency. What has happened is that Congress seeks both to serve as a great coordinate decision-making body *and* at the same time to serve as a negative check on the Presidency.

I would suggest only that this state of affairs cannot continue indefinitely through this exacting century. "When two men ride on a horse," Hobbes said, "one man must ride in front"—and the same may ultimately be true of President and Congress. If ultimately one must give way, I hope that it will be the legislative branch and not the executive. I hope that Congress retains its negative rather than its positive role. I hope that it does this because I think it is best equipped to do this—that is, to serve as a body that investigates, debates, checks, reconsiders, and to some extent vetoes proposals of the President, rather than as a body that tries to work out a series of comprehensive, well-coordinated, and consistent policies. The executive branch, with its single leadership, its relative cohesiveness, and its great reservoir of administrative experience and talent, is best equipped to act as the affirmative policy-making branch. As a mirror—even though a distorted mirror—of the great diversity of interests in the country, Congress should scrutinize and speak up —but it should not act as the central agency of positive government.

This may sound like a radical approach to the role of Congress, but certainly it is not a new idea. Many years ago John Stuart Mill asserted that "Instead of the function of governing for which it is radically unfit, the proper office of representative assembly is to watch and control the government."

Such a conception of the possible role of Congress directly implies the fourth guideline, involving the role of the President. I will be as direct and blunt about this institution as I have been about Congress. I think that the Presidency has become the crucial governmental element in the continued survival and health of the American governmental system. The splendor of the presidential office lies in many things: in the greatness of so many of the men who have occupied the office, including the present incumbent; in the leadership that the President can exercise because of his preeminent position and because of his assured term of power; in the tremendous human and material resources that the presidential office has at its disposal; in the strength and power that the President gains from his many roles, administrative, legislative, ceremonial, military, symbolic; in the dynamic yet intimate relationship between him and the people that is made possible by the press, radio, and television; and finally, in the fact that here in this turbulent, sprawling, ceaselessly changing, tempestuous America is a focal point of order and power and responsibility. Here is an office that the people can hold accountable; here is a man who works amid the bright glare of publicity, who has a chance to strike out on his own but must finally face the people with his record of action or inaction.

The implications of such an evaluation are severalfold. It implies that we must continue to build the office up, rather than cut it down to size, and this means in turn that we must look with some concern on such proposals as the original Bricker Amendment, which would have hobbled presidential power in the crucial area of foreign policy making. It implies that we may wish to reassess the 22nd amendment, which prevents presidential third terms, not only because the amendment gravely reduces the President's power during his second term, but also because it prevents him from going before the voters after his second term and hence impairs his accountability to the people. It means that the people have a right, indeed a duty, to examine fully the implications for the Presidency of President Eisenhower's proposal that he serve four more years in a condition that will prevent his commitment to the grinding toil and tension that the office has traditionally involved.

Do I make too much of the presidential office? Do I expect more from it than any mere mortal in that office can supply? Perhaps. But it is precisely because the office may be superior to the man in it, may demand almost more from him than he can provide, that I look on the Presidency as the ultimate guardian of our security and welfare. For it is an office that elevates the man, provided the man has the potential. It is the office, for example, that took Harry S. Truman, graduate of the Kansas City business school, haberdasher, deacon of the Second Baptist Church, affiliate of the Pendergast machine, county judge, Legionnaire, Shriner, Elk, Moose, Lion, Eagle, United States Senator, and member of the Society for the Preservation and Encouragement of Barber Shop Singing in America, Inc., and made of this mere mortal a President who, whatever his abilities and failings, could make the decision about aid to Europe, and the decision about Korea, and others of the toughest decisions in recent American history.

My fifth guideline involves another key element of our national governmental system, the bureaucracy. Historically America has not treated its bureaucrats too well; it has thrown them out of office when it changed parties; it has underpaid them; worst of all, it has treated them with contempt. In recent years there has been a change for the better; we have freed large areas of the bureaucracy from political pressure through the extension of the merit system; we have improved salaries and working conditions. But we still have a cynical if not disdainful attitude toward the bureaucrats as a whole. This is unfortunate, because they are the people who must administer the tough decisions that governments have to make.

I do not propose that we treat our administrative branch uncritically; indeed, a bit of grumbling and carping at the bureaucracy is doubtless one of the safeguards of the democratic process. I do propose that we treat the bureaucrats more understandingly and sympathetically; more than this, I propose that we continue to search for ways to improve its competence and creativity especially at the top levels. Former President Hoover's recent proposal for a pool of well-paid, carefully selected, top-quality administrators is worth much more consideration than it has received. We might borrow from the French, who have set up impressive systems of recruiting and training administrative talent in their educational system.

I would like to offer a number of other guidelines for consideration in any evaluation of the democratic process. I would like to discuss the Supreme Court and its vital role as guardian of our civil liberties. I would like to discuss the problem of state and local governments and the way that they are meeting—or failing to meet—the social problems of an industrial civilization. But I will forbear. I would conclude on a note that involves all the guidelines that I have offered.

This final suggestion involves the relation of all these governmental institutions, of all these elements of the democratic process, to the people themselves. No Constitution, no government, no bureaucracy can operate effectively and democratically over the long run without constant and extensive participation of the people in the major governmental activities. I do not propose to preach about the need for more civic consciousness, the importance of voting (if you have the right to vote), or taking part more actively in the great game of politics. This advice has been given many times.

I wish only to offer a suggestion that relates to the very heart of the democratic process outside government—namely our party system. In many respects our national political parties are the weakest links in our democratic system. They are badly organized, they are often irresponsible to the people; they often forget their promises to the electorate; they often become more concerned with patronage jobs and petty favors and errand-running than with recruiting the best talent for political leadership or with discussing and posing national issues.

The only way to improve our parties is to take part in them, to wrest control from those who use the parties only for their narrow ends, to convert them into organizations that represent the best in our national political life. They cannot be improved from the outside by preaching at them. This means that those of us interested in doing something about the democratic process must be willing to take part in the drudgery of party activity. This is not only an exacting business, even worse, it is often a boring business. But it is imperative if we wish to strengthen the democratic process.

THE DEMOCRATIC PROCESS

I make a point of the need for party revitalization because I see the party system as the decisive link between the two key guidelines of those that I have discussed earlier—the ultimate good judgment of the people and the vital role of the Presidency. Aside from its many other contributions, a well-organized party system can serve as the connecting rod between popular wishes and presidential action. It can serve as a connecting rod in the sense that the party will respond to popular wishes and at the same time will serve as a mechanism that both propels the President and controls him—as a good connecting rod should. It is a mechanism that, operating efficiently, can give the President the sustained popular backing that he needs to do a good job, but at the same time can prevent him from moving out too far ahead of the people.

I can put this final point best, I think, by saying that we must apply to our re-evaluation of the democratic process today the same kind of imagination and foresight and creativity that the Framers of the Constitution applied to the shaping of our constitutional system 169 years ago. We do not need to tamper with the essential structure of the Constitution that they set up. But we can exercise imagination and boldness and creativity of our own in shaping political institutions that will help make that Constitution more workable under the conditions that face us today and in the future. The Framers planned brilliantly for the future as they saw it; it is our job to carry on that tradition, to subject our democratic process to constant re-evaluation, and to remember always that the democratic process is but a means toward the greater ends of freedom, world stability, and human welfare.

Individual Freedom

The word "freedom" has had some rather curious applications in the history of Western man, but for practical purposes there are two broad approaches to the matter. On the one hand there is the concept of freedom that exists between nations, a set of circumstances that forbids one country from falling under the domination of another. The second concept is the individual freedom, the personal liberty if you choose, of the citizen within a country. It is this latter viewpoint that is under consideration here.

New England's venerable poet, Robert E. Frost, once defined freedom in this manner: "I guess one way of putting it would be you have freedom when you're easy in your harness." America has succeeded, as no other country has, in fashioning a structure of government that allows to the individual a maximum amount of freedom. The harness, in the form of law and the Constitution, has been subject to many strains and stresses in the 170-odd years of its service and there have been times, such as the Civil War period, when it was torn apart. Most of us suspect, however, that

INDIVIDUAL FREEDOM

there are more subtle dangers abroad in the land today, the kind of deterioration that can cause a perfectly good harness to give at the seams. Needless to say, America can ill afford to falter.

As John Knox Jessup recently said: "On America almost alone has fallen the awful responsibility of holding open the door of history against the forces of evil until freedom is born anew all over the world." Our nation developed in a climate of opinion that nourished individualism, courage, and a keen sense of fairness. These attitudes were healthy, positive, and outgoing. Today, individualism appears to be succumbing to pressures of conformity, courage giving ground before all kinds of fear, and the presumption of innocence has largely been subverted by assumptions of guilt. America cannot hold the door open much longer with this kind of muscle.

But there's something more involved than mere endurance and the ultimate test lies in our ability to act intelligently after the issues and trends have been properly isolated and evaluated. Few men in the country today are better qualified to comment on "individual freedom" than Henry Steele Commager, who is widely recognized as one of America's outstanding historians.

INDIVIDUAL FREEDOM

A native of Pittsburgh, Pennsylvania, Dr. Commager received his education at the University of Chicago and the University of Copenhagen. Prior to accepting a professorship in history at Columbia University in 1939, he was on the faculty at New York University for thirteen years. He was visiting lecturer in American History at Cambridge University (England) in 1942 and again in 1948. In this country he has presented lectures at the University of California, Harvard, Duke, Boston University, University of Virginia, Dartmouth, and the University of Chicago. This type of schedule alone has been the despair of many good men. But Dr. Commager's vigor and ability carry far beyond the classroom and it is through the medium of his books and many articles contributed to the press that a whole generation of students have come to feel the influence of his thought on American civilization.

In 1930 Dr. Commager collaborated with Samuel Eliot Morison on *The Growth of the American Republic,* a two-volume study that remains today one of the most widely used college textbooks on American History. A biography of Theodore Parker, *America: The Story of a Free People; Documents of American History; The American Mind; Majority Rule and Minority Rights;* and *The Blue and the Grey*—these are some of the books he has written. Last year, the Oxford University Press published one of his latest works called, *Freedom, Loyalty, Dissent,* a title that logically introduces the topic of this essay.

This essay has been drawn from an address called "The Nature of American Freedom" which Dr. Commager delivered at the Schwenkfelder Library in May, 1954.

INDIVIDUAL FREEDOM

by Henry Steele Commager

IT IS MY intention to deal with what, for want of a better term, I have called the pattern or the nature of American freedom. Before I attempt to delineate that pattern, analyze that nature, a qualifying word, and that is, that while it is perfectly natural for us to speak in terms of American freedom, we must beware of the temptation to think too exclusively in terms of *American* freedom. We must beware of that temptation which assails us now, perhaps more strongly than at any previous time, to suppose that we somehow discovered freedom and that we have a monopoly on it— an attitude associated with that dangerous notion that, lo, we are the people and all wisdom dies with us. We must realize that freedom is something that concerns the whole of mankind, not just our own people, and that any exclusive or chauvinistic, or parochial approach to it will do grave harm rather than advantage to ourselves and to the peoples of the world.

We have carried freedom farther in some respects than have other nations. In some respects we lag behind other peoples. But we certainly do not have a monopoly on it and it does not become us to assume that we can pose before the world as teachers of all aspects of freedom, to explain to the English, for example, or the Scandinavians, the true nature of freedom. They know something about it themselves. And we must be on guard against that constant temptation to spiritual pride; the sort of thing that would have us suppose that only in America do mothers love their babies, or boys go to school, or any of the other pleasant things happen. We must beware of a too exclusive and narrow interpretation of this great concept and realize that what we have of freedom we share, and that only on the basis of sharing can we ourselves maintain it, and be secure with it.

The first thing we note when we turn to an examination of the nature of freedom in America, is that by great good fortune—by providential intervention if you will—freedom in America has from the beginning been constructive and creative. Freedom has not needed to operate as it had to operate in most old world countries, primarily in a negative fashion. We did not need to turn first to the great task of overthrowing things before we could turn to the even greater task of re-establishing and re-creating them. We did not have in this new world, a powerful monarchy, a king claiming divine right. We did not have an established church, for the established churches of the colonies

INDIVIDUAL FREEDOM

were too weak to be dangerous. We did not have an aristocracy that had to be overthrown. We did not have a great military caste, dedicated to warfare and conquest. We did not have a class system. We could start almost with a clean slate. We could start at once with the great constructive tasks of freedom, start to build, start by addressing ourselves to particular things like the extension of the suffrage, the establishment of a system of popular education, the achievement of equality, economic and social, the widespread distribution of land—a whole series of social and humanitarian reform programs.

There is, to be sure, one notable exception here, that is the exception of freedom for the black man. That had to be fought for over a long period of years, and finally won only by the greatest civil war of the nineteenth century. Because freedom for the black man was won in this fashion, it left after it a heritage of misunderstanding and bitterness which is still very much with us. But just suppose we had had to fight for religious freedom in the same way! Or suppose we had had to vindicate self-government against a King or against an aristocracy in the same fashion, seeking—as Jefferson said of the old world man in his first inaugural—"seeking through blood and slaughter his long lost liberty."

It is of utmost importance that Americans retain this

characteristic of freedom as something constructive and creative, and that we be everlastingly on guard against the insidious notion that freedom is negative, that freedom is the preservation of the status quo, that freedom is something which existed in the past, that we have exhausted its possibilities, that it has no future but only a history. Freedom has been creative in the past, it is creative today, and it must be creative in the future. It must be freedom *for* things, not freedom *against* them. It must be freedom in terms of developing new potentialities, of releasing the fullest possibilities of a democracy.

In the second place freedom in America has been voluntaristic and associational. It originated in voluntary practices and activities in society. It has not come from above, it has come from below. It has made its way by men and women getting together and doing things: setting up a church, setting up a town, setting up a state, pushing through a reform—abolition or woman suffrage. It has functioned through voluntary associations and the private voluntary association has put its imprint on the whole character of freedom in America from the very earliest days—from the Pilgrims and the Puritans coming together voluntarily, setting up churches, not needing bishops or kings to permit it —then transforming the churches into communities, and into states; setting up their colleges, setting up

INDIVIDUAL FREEDOM

other institutions of enlightenment and of grace. The first approach to a national government in America in 1774 was prophetically called "The Association." And the notion of association and doing things through association characterized American democracy and American freedom from the beginning.

Every church in America, every political party, every reform organization, most schools and colleges (until recent years), all professional societies, and all fraternal orders are private voluntary associations. Look where you will, our country is criss-crossed and bound together by the activities of these voluntary associations. These have been the instruments whereby men and women realized the meaning of freedom in America, freedom of religions, education, reform, and social activities.

This has been characteristic above all of the English speaking peoples, and of all the English speaking peoples especially of the American people, this notion that freedom comes from below, from men and women working together. Freedom is created day by day out of the multifarious activities of millions of men and women working together in their organizations and associations. It does not come out of a series of abstractions or theories or doctrines, but out of the functional activities of society.

Again, need I suggest that the very principle of

voluntary association is today suspect and that the practices are being discouraged even from official sources and that the rise of the odious doctrine of "guilt by association" imperils the principles and the practice of voluntary association. And need I remind you that the same principle that is applied to so called "left wing" organizations may be applied to central or to right wing organizations or to any organization whatsoever, and that once the habit of joining is discouraged, once the young are taught that it is better not to join than to join, they will not only cease joining dangerous organizations, they will cease joining political parties, churches, and fraternal organizations as well; they will in fact lose the habit of joining. Tocqueville saw this over a century ago, and warned against it in one of the most memorable chapters of his great book *Democracy in America*. What he said at that time has been proved true in our own days.

In the third place freedom in America has tended to be amelioristic and reformist. It has not been content with the status quo but has attempted constantly to improve on what was there. Philosophically freedom in America has rested on two assumptions: the assumption of the perfectability of the individual man and of society, and the assumption of progress. Now, neither of these assumptions can be proved. But the notions that men have within them some portion of divinity, that they can work towards perfection, and that society itself is susceptible of indefinite improvement—these notions are so deeply imbedded in the American experience and ingrained in the American character that it is inconceivable that we should be able to dispense with them.

It is a very serious matter therefore if we cease to believe in progress or in the natural goodness of man and to take that as a working hypothesis. For in our own history, the hypothesis of the goodness of man, in the improvability of society have in large part justified themselves. We should not too easily give up faith in progress and perfectability or abandon that fervor for reform which has characterized us in the past. We should not give way to complacency and smugness or to supposing that we have found the answers to all questions.

In the fourth place freedom in America has been pluralistic. It has never been set in a single uniform pattern, but always in a multiform and variegated pattern. Again, this is not because of any peculiar virtue in the American people, or because we decided on this policy from the beginning. It is rather an accident of history, because in the very beginning peoples of all the Western world poured into America, bringing with them their varied cultures and languages and faiths: when the British took over New Amsterdam they found twenty-four languages spoken on that island. From the very beginning there was a pattern of color, race, language, and religious denominationalism as variegated as we have at the present time. Almost everything about our history has followed a pluralistic fashion. The federal system, is of course, a monument to political pluralism and to the motion of experimentation within the framework of the states. Our religious pattern is pluralistic with some 250 to 300 religious denominations all flourishing side by side. Our school system, with its combination of the private and the public, is to a lesser degree, a monument to the principle of pluralism, but anything as obvious as this does not need elaboration.

Pluralism was the price we had to pay for unity, and unity has come to America by permitting diversity and pluralism to flourish. Those great men who chose the American motto, *E Pluribus Unum,* Jefferson, John Adams, and Franklin, chose better even than they knew. Out of plurality has come unity; within unity there is plurality. In America unity has grown from within, the only way it can ever really grow.

Pluralism, then, was an essential element in unity. On no other terms could America have achieved what she did achieve, that is, national unity over a continental domain. We think of America in terms of a single nation but we should think of it in terms of

Europe, or of South America. Why after all did we not turn out like South America, twenty nations instead of one? We have as many geographical regions, as many economic interests, as many climates as South America, a more heterogeneous population, and a more varied religious scene.

How did we achieve unity? We achieved it by not trying to thrust it down the throats of our people, by not imposing it from above. We achieved it by allowing it to grow, as it grows in any sound and healthy society—in church, school, or fraternal organization. You cannot impose it any more than you can impose honor, any more than you can impose grace. One of the dangers of our day is that we forget this elementary lesson—a lesson we should have learned well in 300 years—and take refuge in a superimposed unity and loyalty. But that kind of unity will not work in the long run.

A fifth characteristic of freedom closely allied with this fourth is that it has been experimental and pragmatic. Again this is something imposed upon us by historical experience, rather than something which we chose. From the beginning everything about our country was an experiment, and what we are is the product of a thousand experiments, great and small. The new world itself was the greatest experiment—the gamble of settling an unknown continent. The idea that men might govern themselves was an experiment; the idea of the separation of church and state was an experiment; the ideas of republicanism, of democracy, of equality, of federalism, were experiments, and so too the political party, the written constitution, the notion of colonies as equals—all these were experiments, all these were something new under the sun. The generation that founded the republic embarked upon these experiments with stout heart and good faith and carried them through to a successful conclusion. And our tremendous prosperity, our high standard of living, our widespread enlightenment are, to a large degree, the result of a series of successful experiments.

An experiment requires, of course, that people are dissatisfied with what they have and want something new, that they think they can do something better than has been done in the past—make a better plow, or make a better constitution, or a better church. Experimentalism requires boldness and audacity, the faith that there are new worlds to conquer in every field of thought and of endeavor.

In the sixth place, freedom in America has functioned through private enterprise. I need not remind you of the role of private enterprise in the establishment of the nation and of the continuing function of private enterprise in our history. The enterprise that brought the first settlers to Virginia and to the Bay

INDIVIDUAL FREEDOM

Colony, and to a score of other places in colonies, continued, as we sometimes forget, to bring hundreds of thousands and millions, and eventually tens of millions of persons from other shores to the New World to start up again.

It is, however, a grave injustice to our history and to our people to suppose that the concept of private enterprise is exclusively or primarily an economic concept. There is private enterprise in the economy to be sure, but it is distinctly secondary, for without enterprise in the minds and spirit of men you get no enterprise anywhere else. Private enterprise begins with the individual, with the individual mind and spirit. It begins with someone somewhere challenging the existing system and trying to improve it, trying to make a better church, or a better school, or a better political system. The only enterprise that counts, in the long run, is the enterprise in the minds of men. If that is discouraged or smothered, enterprise in the economic field will not last very long. This elementary lesson every totalitarian government has known, and every totalitarian government has begun not by controlling the economy, but by controlling the schools, the universities, the radio, the press, the libraries, the scientists, knowing full well that once those whose function it was to criticize and to challenge were silenced, it would be an easy matter to control any other institution whatsoever in the society or the economy.

We must rescue and restore this noble concept of private enterprise to the realm where it has real meaning and where it has work to do. We must restore it to the realm of intellectual activity, to the laboratory, the library, the schoolroom, and the platform. This is the kind of enterprise our nation needs if it is to continue along the road of freedom. One of the great dangers that confronts us is the notion that private enterprise can flourish in economies or in politics if it does not flourish in the intellectual or the spiritual realms.

Closely associated with this matter of private enterprise is the problem of relation between government and freedom—a very old issue and a very modern issue. The reconciliation of liberty and order is in one sense the greatest problem in the whole realm of government. Those wise and virtuous men who established the American constitutional system gave a great deal of thought to this question of the relation of government to freedom. They knew that, on the one hand, government must be powerful enough to protect men and women in their freedom, that it had a positive and constructive role to play, and they assigned to government ample powers to do all those things that government needs to do: to protect the nation abroad and at home, to preserve the natural resources of the nation that are the heritage of no one generation but of all generations; to preserve those resources from the ravages of particular states or particular individual groups and preserve them for the whole nation and for all groups. They knew that freedom can be threatened as much from the abandonment of governmental power as from the excess of governmental power and that if freedom is to flourish, to be applied to creative and constructive purposes, government must be strong enough to preserve peace and order and advance the general welfare. An impotent government is as dangerous as an overpowerful government.

The framers gave ample powers to government, but they also established firm restraints on government. They knew that there were certain areas where government should not and could not operate. They knew that if liberty was to be reconciled with authority, government must not only be endowed with ample powers to govern, but must be effectively circumscribed in areas where it has no business whatsoever to function. What were those areas? They are all set forth clearly enough in the Constitution. Thus it is clear that government had no business whatsoever in the control of ideas, in religion, in the press, in speech, in assembly, or association.

The area placed outside the scope of government by state and federal constitutions alike, was that of the communication of thought. A grave danger confronts us now if government indirectly, or directly, enters these forbidden fields, invades those areas where government is, by very nature, incompetent to operate. By direct activity I have reference to the activities of Congressional investigating committees and their associated organizations—to their efforts to set up standards of what is orthodox in religion, or in education or in the field of literature. The framers of our Constitutional system, and successive generations thereafter, knew that these things were things that government is incompetent to deal with and knew that a government which attempted to deal with them would imperil the liberty of society. We must beware now lest we abandon our well-established and fully vindicated view of the nature of governmental power and the nature of the limitations on governmental power.

Government freedom in America has always relied on public education, and dependence on education is the eighth characteristic of American freedom. No other country has a comparable story to tell. The spectacle of a handful of colonists, months away from civilization, fighting for their very existence and not knowing from day to day whether their society would survive, yet resolutely establishing the Boston Latin School and Harvard College, and then passing the first law in all history requiring every community to support public schools, the laws of 1642 and 1647—such a historical experience is one to fill every American with gratification. Throughout our history, unevenly to be sure, and with many vicissitudes, Americans have reaffirmed their faith in education. The fathers of the Revolutionary and the Constitutional period were profoundly convinced that only an enlightened electorate could make democracy work.

Thomas Jefferson, the foremost prophet and spokesman of democracy, was all his life an educator. Beginning his career with an attempt to reform the whole educational system of Virginia, he ended it as the father of the University of Virginia (that University was as you know the extended shadow of one man). His interest was typical, in an exaggerated sense to be sure, of the passion with which his generation regarded education. For this generation, fighting for its life, found time to set up seven new colleges and state universities during time of war, so at the end of the war when we became an independent nation we had more colleges than Britain and more students in universities and colleges than any other country. This generation found time to write into the fundamental laws subsidies of public education by land grants.

We know that the demands upon our educational system are greater today than they ever were, and that the dangers from irrationalism too are greater today than they ever were. We do not face today any philosophical repudiation for the claims of education but we do face two very serious dangers. One, a purely material one, is a failure to appreciate the magnitude of the responsibility of educating this next generation —an unwillingness to make the sacrifices called for, to build and staff and maintain an adequate educational system. Remember that wonderful line in the Northwest Ordinance, "Schools and knowledge, being necessary to the happiness of mankind, education and the means thereof shall forever be encouraged." Yet we spend a smaller percentage of the national income on schools today than we did in the year 1900. But we are already in process of remedying this. Perhaps more serious is the development of a climate of opinion in which education can with difficulty carry on its beneficent work. That is a climate of opinion which uses a phrase like "brain trust" as a term of opprobrium; which permits a presidential candidate to speak disparagingly of his opponent as having a "Harvard accent"; which either fears or mistrusts its teachers, scholars, scientists, men of letters, and artists. It is not yet a pervasive climate, but it is alarmingly widespread. We must restore what we have had in the past—faith and confidence in the processes of education. We must restore an atmosphere which encourages educators to operate as effectively as they can, without intimidation or fear. We must maintain, at all costs, freedom for

INDIVIDUAL FREEDOM

the schools, for libraries, for laboratories, for foundations, freedom for all institutions dedicated to the search for truth. For only if we guarantee freedom to these can they hope to achieve their great end, of discovering and developing the possibilities of truth.

Finally, freedom in America has from the beginning had a sense of mission. It has been a gospel to be carried throughout the world. In a Jefferson, a Washington, a Lincoln, this took a magnanimous form. In less farsighted people, it took the far from magnanimous form of manifest destiny. Yet, there was less of that, perhaps, with us than with most people. What has characterized us in the past is a sense of obligation, a feeling that ours was a testing ground—that all mankind was looking upon us to see whether our experiments would work, that we had a peculiar obligation therefore to see that democracy and freedom did work. Ours was, said Jefferson, "the world's last, best hope." It was, said Lincoln, "the last best hope of earth." This notion that America was, as Turgot put it, the hope of the human race, is something, which can be made to look a bit fatuous, but which is deeply ingrained in our experience. I think it has given us a feeling of responsibility which on the whole has been good for us, and for others.

There is a very moving passage in William Wetmore Story's life of his father, Justice Story of the United

States Supreme Court. Story was not only Justice of the Supreme Court but many other things besides, for living as he did in the days before labor-saving devices he had time to have three or four careers instead of one. He was a professor at the Harvard Law School, the author of some twenty volumes of commentaries, and active in politics, and in the cultural and religious life of his day. William Wetmore Story tells of his father's last lecture to the Harvard Law School:

> As my father took his seat to commence the exercises this fact (that it was the last meeting) seemed to strike his mind and he began by alluding to it. Moved, as he proceeded, by the train of thought and feeling thus accidentally set in motion, he slid into a glowing discourse upon the principles and objects of the Constitution, the views of the great men of the Revolution by whom it was drawn, the position of our country, the dangers to which it was exposed, and the duty of every citizen to see that the republic sustained no detriment. He spoke as he went on of the hopes for freedom with which America was originated, of the anxious eyes that watched this progress, of the voices that called from land to land to inquire of its welfare, closing in an exhortation to the students to labor for the furtherance of justice and free principles, to expand,

deepen and liberalize the law, to discard all low and ambitious motives and to seek in all their public acts to establish the foundations of right and truth.

I need not add that our own generation must, of necessity, have a greater sense of obligation than any previous generation. For upon us have fallen obligations heavier even than those that confronted the generation of Jefferson, or of Story, or of Lincoln. We are today, through no will of our own, the leader of the free world. As Mr. Jessup has said, "on America almost alone has fallen the awful responsibility of holding open the door of history against the forces of evil until freedom is born anew all over the world." We are not so much animated by a sense of missionary activity as by a grave and sobering feeling that upon us rests in the last analysis, the success or failure of the experiment of freedom. The rest of the world looks to us to salvage freedom and to protect it against its enemies and we must at all cost justify that faith. We cannot maintain or exercise leadership in the cause of freedom if we do not have leadership. We cannot expect other nations to trust our leadership if we do not trust it ourselves. We cannot command the support and the confidence of our fellow nations and our associates in the struggle for peace if we ourselves conspicuously lack faith and confidence. We cannot expect to command confidence at home or abroad if we substitute for the processes of reason, the processes of unreason; if we substitute for the vocabulary of reasoned argument the vocabulary of Billingsgate; if we conduct our politics, not with a view to great and noble ends but to partisan and shabby ends; if we create an atmosphere of suspicion and hatred and vilification; if we try to conduct our great affairs by charges and counter charges of treason and near treason, of subversion and disloyalty. We must restore to our public life that atmosphere of confidence, harmony and decency without which, as Jefferson said, "Liberty and life itself are but dreary things." We must recapture something of those high purposes which animated us not too long ago as we saved the Western World for freedom. We must emancipate ourselves from this unprecedented and unworthy development of recent years, where every man eyes his neighbor with suspicion and fear. For in an atmosphere of fear and suspicion, no great tasks can be performed. In a society which dwarfs its men no great men will emerge to perform a man's task. Only faith can do the great constructive and creative work which we are called upon to do. In the words of the great architect of victory, "let us move forward with strong and active faith."

World Peace

Ever since America entered the uncharted seas of the atomic age, world peace has been of paramount importance to all humankind. Surely, it is the supreme question of our time and with just cause we are an age of Americans deeply convinced that the world is in a critical state. International tensions of the first magnitude are now accompanied by fantastic forces of evil and destruction. There has been a certain authenticity and finality about some recent explosions that will not be denied. One wishes, rather wistfully, that the scientists would lay down their slide rules and turn off their cyclotrons while twentieth-century man—to borrow a phrase—crawls up on the shore and rests until his better moral half overtakes him.

To be sure, civilization has survived some rather acute crises in the past, but as a source of comfort, this fact alone leaves much to be desired. It is quite a simple matter to look down upon the tarnished coin of human nature and read that man will always quarrel, that forces of violence are concomitant to life itself. And yet, the philosopher will turn over this coin and on the bright side take note of man's impelling will to peace. The coin is once again spinning madly and we can be forgiven if we await the outcome with dismay.

A personal position with respect to this problem is largely a matter of temperament—it may range from mild irritation to despair, but it won't go away. Thus, all Americans have thought rather seriously about world peace, but on too many occasions we have thrown up our hands and determined to leave the matter to wiser heads. And yet, as Americans, we must force our minds to get on a sound program for peace. We have to coddle and nourish a sense of critical responsibility that will at once preserve and carry forward as a mighty force the heritage that America defends. To this end we will need broad knowledge, sound judgment, and deep faith.

Joseph Esrey Johnson was born in Longdale, Virginia. A graduate of Harvard University, he taught history at Williams College before and after World War II. His tenure with the Department of State began in 1942. Acting Chief of the State Department's Division of International Security Affairs for a year, Dr. Johnson became head of the Division in 1945. He was an adviser to the United States delegations to the Dumbarton Oaks Conference in 1944 and the Inter-American Conference on Problems of War and Peace held in Mexico in 1945, and was an expert on the United States delegation to the United Nations Conference on International Organization at San Francisco later that year. In 1946 he served as adviser to the United States Delegation to the General Assembly of the United Nations and to the United States Representative in the United Nations Security Council, both in London and New York. In 1947 he was a member of the Department of State's Policy Planning Staff, and in 1948 Deputy United States Representative on the Interim Committee of the United Nations General Assembly.

This is the splendid record which led to his appointment as President of the Carnegie Endowment for International Peace in 1950. Dr. Johnson presented the thoughts on world peace that constitute this essay in lecture form in March, 1954.

WORLD PEACE

by Joseph E. Johnson

THE fact that we have been successful in our attempts to create thermonuclear explosions shows that we now face a challenge, not alone to American life but to life itself. Recently, a very great man of our time, commenting on the fact that thermonuclear weapons were now being developed and that it might be possible, before too long, to transmit thermonuclear weapons by guided missile, remarked in a style that may easily be recognized even though I do not mention him by name: "It now appears possible to eliminate the human race without risking the life of a single aviator." That remark points up a situation worth very serious thought, one about which I have thought a great deal since I first heard it.

The news of the continuing experiments in the West and in the Pacific give poignant meaning to words which Secretary of State Dulles spoke before the United Nations General Assembly in 1953 and to Mr. Eisenhower's own dramatic statement before the same body three months later. What Mr. Dulles said, in a fine speech, was:

Joseph E. Johnson

Physical scientists have now found means which, if they are developed, can wipe life off the surface of this planet.

These words that I speak are words that can be taken literally. The destructive power inherent in matter must be controlled by the idealism of the spirit and the wisdom of the mind. They alone stand between us and a lifeless planet.

There are plenty of problems in this world, many of them interconnected. But there is no problem which compares with this central, universal problem of saving the human race from extinction.

Mr. Dulles was, of course, referring to so-called atomic bombs, to hydrogen bombs, and, one would guess from reports in the press, to cobalt bombs. Now, no one can possibly tell today whether the most destructive weapons will be used if a Third World War should break out. But we can be reasonably certain that the so-called simple A-bomb will be used if war comes, and we should be guilty of very bad planning were we to assume that the other nations will not use atomic weapons, even though we may hope and pray that they will not, and that they will be a "deterrent," as Anthony Eden suggested, to the outbreak of the Third World War.

And it may be well to reflect for a moment on what

tremendous developments have taken place in just a few years, developments that permit the bomb exploded at Hiroshima to be characterized as a "simple device" possessing only 1/600th of the power of the device that was exploded last year. But the point is that world peace does become a challenge to life on this earth, not just to American life. Mr. Dulles' closing words about the importance of this problem can therefore, I believe, constitute my text.

As a former historian, I hesitate to say that any of the great challenges to this country is the principal one, is the greatest of all. And yet I find it difficult, as Mr. Dulles obviously does, to comprehend a greater one. This problem is a very special challenge to America, to our way of life, to our constitutional political system, to our ideas, to the ideals and spiritual values which we have developed and cherished. It seems to me to be a special challenge to Americans for three reasons.

The first of these is the simple one—that we possess the weapons. Of course it is known that the Soviet Union has atomic bombs and has discovered the secret of thermonuclear reactions. It is known also that Great Britain has atomic weapons; nevertheless there is good reason to believe that we have more atomic capacity than any other country, and it is likely that

Joseph E. Johnson

we shall remain in the lead. I may say that I fervently hope that we do, unless and until we see that we can achieve some means of bringing about a reduction and control of atomic power. This likelihood of our remaining in the lead is, however, no cause for complacency, nor even cause for much assurance. For when a potential enemy, which the Soviet Union has in effect proclaimed itself to be—an enemy which can move without warning—possesses the capacity to knock us out, it does not really matter a great deal that we should be able to knock them out five or ten times over. On the contrary, our possession of atomic superiority give us added responsibilities, magnifies the challenge. Having these weapons and having the means to deliver them, we could be tempted to rely much too heavily on one weapon; we could be tempted to "throw our weight around." We could be very easily tempted—and this is a matter which must concern all of us very deeply—to play down moral considerations, overlook the moral aspects of the possession of this terrible weapon. We could be tempted to become "trigger happy."

This weapon also creates a problem for us in decision-making, a problem new in our experience. Who should decide when to use these weapons, if ever, and how, and in consultation with whom? Under the law, the President of the United States now has the authority to make the decision, but that does not make these rhetorical questions. For the responsibilities which go with that authority are truly awful, and the President could not, and would not, make the decision alone without wide consultation. Furthermore, important constitutional issues are involved because obviously the use of an atomic weapon, if Congress had not declared war, would raise questions of the deepest significance involving the relationship between the executive and the legislative, as well as questions of timing. We must not forget as we think about problems of war and peace that the time factor has changed immeasurably. To cite just one example: in Korea in June 1950, the prevention of the North Koreans from overrunning the whole of South Korea was a matter of hours; our government was forced to act before it could get what would have been desirable authorization from the United Nations Security Council. The authorization, otherwise, might have come too late.

There is another problem arising from this bitter business of decision-making involving the weapon, and that is the problem of relationships with our allies, whom we need and who need us. You will recall that Mr. Truman made an ill-considered remark in November 1950 about the possibility of using the atomic weapon. Within forty-eight hours Prime Minister Attlee was on his way to Washington to find out

Joseph E. Johnson

exactly what Mr. Truman had meant. You may recall also that in 1954 the Canadian Secretary of State for External Affairs, Lester Pearson, in Washington, made some comments about the doctrine of instant retaliation, which Mr. Dulles had expressed in January.

This leads me to the second reason why the challenge is a special one to Americans. We are the leaders of the free world, not because we wish to be—for indeed many of us do not like our position—but because we cannot escape history. Leaders of free men face special difficulties that do not exist for the slave-drivers of totalitarian states. Leaders of free men cannot lead by fear and compulsion. They must inspire confidence and gain consent. We as a people, and our political leaders, have, by and large, learned how this is done inside our own country and under our own Constitution. But the task is, inherently, infinitely harder in the complex world of foreign affairs, and we are beginners at it.

The third reason for the special challenge is the newness of the situation. It is new in two senses. The need for peace is greater than ever before, and the challenge of peace is really quite new to the American people and their government. Let me elaborate these points individually.

The peace movement has a long history. Men have known and said for centuries that war is bad, that war is morally wrong. Men have always sought ways to eliminate war. But the movement picked up force during and after the Napoleonic wars, again at the end of the nineteenth century, and even more vigorously after the First World War. Still, it never attracted a great deal of attention from the ordinary citizen. For example: Mr. Carnegie founded his Endowment for International Peace in 1910 for the purpose of, as he put it, hastening "the abolition of international war, the foulest blot upon our civilization." Although he got a number of statesmen and others to support him in this movement, the impact on society as a whole was not very heavy.

In August 1945 this problem of peace acquired real urgency. Not until then could a man say, as Einstein is reported to have said, that though he did not know precisely what weapons would be used in World War Three, he was sure of those which would be employed in World War Four—"rocks."

The challenge of peace, then, has a new quality about it today. And yet it is my own position, my own view, and I state this even though I am the head of an organization concerned primarily with finding ways to peace, that peace is not even today the first and highest goal. It is not the aim to which I give the highest priority. I place freedom and justice higher on my own personal scale of values, and I suspect that most other thinking Americans do too. Their loss would, in my opinion, be much too high a price to pay for peace, even in an atomic age.

The other respect in which the situation is new, relates specifically to American life. Taking our history as a whole, the dangers of war, even of world war, have never, before the last decade, appeared very serious to Americans. There was, to be sure, a moment in 1919 and 1920 when it appeared that we did think the dangers of war were important. But we rejected the League of Nations, and this rejection seems to me a manifestation of a lack of real concern in this country over problems of peace and war. In our earliest days we even gained from war. The action of France in 1778, which changed a domestic conflict inside the British Empire into a war fought all over the world, made our independence possible. And for the next forty years we pursued a policy based upon the conviction, in Jefferson's words, "that Europe's distress was America's gain." This policy was of long-run benefit, despite the distresses of an undeclared war against France at the end of the eighteenth century, and a declared war against Britain from 1812 to 1815. The wars of others made it possible for the United States to get at a bargain such things as the Louisiana Territory, stretching from Baton Rouge, Louisiana, to Boseman, Montana, from Pueblo, Colorado, to St. Paul, Minnesota.

WORLD PEACE

When, after the Treaty of Ghent in 1815 and the proclamation of the Monroe Doctrine in 1823, we contentedly settled down to cultivate our own vast garden and enlarge it in suitable ways, ignoring a Europe at peace, the problem of world peace concerned most Americans not at all; they even, on two occasions a half-century apart, showed so little respect for peace itself that they went to war almost lightheartedly against Mexico in 1846 and against Spain in 1898.

Now, however, our security is gone and we know, most of us, that problems of peace and war are a matter of direct concern not only to our government but to us as individuals. Americans in uniform—just imagine anybody saying this fifteen years ago!—Americans in uniform are in Korea and Okinawa, in Wiesbaden and in Salzburg; in Morocco, Turkey, and Indo-China.

The Vice President of the United States made a journey around the world, and the Secretary of State has while in office visited every continent but Australia on missions involving problems of war and peace. We all know these things, but it sometimes helps to bring them down to cases to demonstrate the change from only a short time ago. As recently as 1939 a leading senator, William E. Borah, the most powerful individual on the Senate Foreign Relations Committee, boasted of the fact that he had never been abroad!

Joseph E. Johnson

So much for the special aspects of the challenge to Americans. What about the nature of this challenge? It confronts us, and we know it. What is its nature, what are its component parts? The first thing to be said about it is that it is going to last a long time. Mr. Carnegie provided, in his deed of gift for the Carnegie Endowment, that after world peace had been achieved, the funds of the Carnegie Endowment should be employed for other purposes, for the next most important problem of the world, but I assure you I have no expectation that permanent peace will throw me out of employment before I reach the retirement stage. Of course, the Marxist would argue that I am bound to be a warmonger, because, according to Marxist doctrine, economic interest determines actions and, since it is clearly to my interest to stay in a good job, I am bound to work against peace. Even so, I say that the challenge is a long one. There is no easy way to meet it, and we shall have to have stamina if we are to last the course. We cannot find slick or trick solutions. Peace is not brought about by gimmicks.

The most obvious element of this challenge is the threat presented by the policy of the Kremlin. In 1946, Dean Acheson, then Under-Secretary of State, called this policy "aggressive and expanding." In 1954, Secretary of State John Foster Dulles, in an article which was published in *Foreign Affairs* magazine, said—and he used almost exactly the very same words: "It is still aggressive and still expansive." A group of men who command a center of great power have announced by word, and demonstrated by deed, the determination to destroy by every means available to them, the values that we hold dear and the institutions which defend and foster those values. These men are our acknowledged enemies, and as Mr. Dulles pointed out, the Berlin Conference of February 1954, if it showed nothing else, revealed clearly that any hopes of a change with the death of Stalin were hopes without basis in fact.

The challenge to us is to meet these enemies, to frustrate them, to turn them back, and in doing so to avoid a Third World War on the one hand, and to protect our values and institutions on the other. There is no good in stopping aggression abroad and succumbing to tyranny at home. If we succumb to the kinds of violations of our rights and freedoms which certain people in high places are guilty of at the present time, it will not really matter much if the Communists beat us or not. What profiteth America if she gain the whole world and lose her own soul?

The second and, to most of us, less obvious part of the challenge, is itself twofold. It is, on the one hand, the problem of preventing clashes throughout the world from becoming small wars, and small wars from setting off large ones, like sparks in a powder keg. And,

Joseph E. Johnson

on the other hand, it is the problem of seeking to promote that hardest of all processes in international life—peaceful change.

Change is a fact of international life and of national life. As a historian, the only thing I am certain of is that change is permanent. We have means inside our government for bringing about peaceful change; we take care of change by legislative action, by administrative action, by constitutional interpretation, by the give-and-take that goes on constantly in our relations with each other.

On the international scene, we have no such ready and good machinery. The Charter of the United Nations makes a brief reference to peaceful change, but there is no spelling out of how it is to be brought about. And conflicts resulting from change do exist on the international scene. Look at Palestine, Kashmir, Morocco, Indo-China, Korea, South Africa; you can go right around the world and find signs of conflict. It is unrealistic to hope that bloodshed can always be avoided. We as the leaders of the non-Communist world must ride these changes, guide them, and try to control them, or we shall be overwhelmed by them. And, parenthetically, one of the toughest problems we are going to face emotionally is that of learning that we can not do this and expect everybody to like us. The British succeeded quite well in doing many things in a less difficult world, but they never quite succeeded in making everybody like what they did. To take one current example: how can we deal with the Moroccan question without getting either the Moroccans and the Arab world, or the French, or perhaps both, to dislike us? Our best hope, in my opinion, is that we may succeed in avoiding the creation of *unnecessary* causes for dislike.

This aspect of the challenge, this problem of helping to bring about change without creating major conflicts, relates especially to those areas which are now, or recently have been, colonial; to India, to Indonesia, to the Philippines, to Kenya, to Morocco, to Tunis, to Iran, to British Honduras, to Guatemala. Name your continent, name your place. In most of these countries, there are two forces marching side by side. One is the demand for enough to eat and a chance to live a life. We Americans forget that in a country like India average life expectancy is twenty-seven years. We forget that of three hundred and fifty million Indians there are probably no more than three or four million who have ever had a full meal in their whole lives. These people have learned, largely from the West, that this is not foreordained, that they no longer have to endure such suffering. The West has demonstrated that people do not have to die young, that their wives do not have to die in childbirth, that

Joseph E. Johnson

their babies do not have to die at the age of a year or two, that they do not have to go hungry. The people of Asia have learned this, and they are going to insist on the same thing for themselves.

At the same time—and this is the other facet of the situation, the other force—they have learned from us of the advantages of self-government. They are nationalists, they are not going to be governed by others.

This development has been called "the Hundred Year Revolution." I think that is a fair description. I would remind you that it began long before Lenin and Trotsky seized power in Moscow in November of 1917, and it will go on, I hope, after their successors have lost power in Moscow. Dealing with this revolution is perhaps the greatest, the most stimulating of the tasks which we face. We must act as midwives to the birth of a new world, and in doing so preserve the life of both mother and child. The challenge calls for courage, imagination, skill, and a great deal of that generosity for which Americans are justly renowned.

The last element of the challenge I shall only mention because I have already referred to it in another context—that is the challenge to our leadership which is presented by all these multifarious problems.

What do we need to do, and what have we done in the way of responding?

It seems to me that the first thing we have to do is

to embark upon a very searching re-examination of ourselves and of some of the convictions that we hold. There is need for the hardest kind of hard thought, not only on the part of American leaders, but on the part of all Americans because—and I am sure you will have gathered this even though I have not said it specifically—we Americans in our democracy are going to have to find the answers ourselves and not have them given to us solely by our leaders.

I should like to mention two of the areas in which we must engage in some of this bold thinking. The first relates to the nature of peace and war. Heretofore we have tended to think of peace and war as two sides of the same coin. It lies on the table peace side up; somebody declares war and presto, it flips over to war. In due course the war ends, the coin is flipped again, a treaty is signed, and peace reigns. That is a pleasantly easy way to look at the question, but does the world we live in fit this picture?

I suggest we change our image and think of something like a spectrum, with the violet of peaceful existence and amity on one end and the red of total war on the other. In between there would be differing degrees of political, economic, and psychological pressure. There would be hidden aggression, threats of force, "cold war," military incidents, little border shooting matches, police actions, small wars, wars be-

Joseph E. Johnson

tween great powers which yet lack the character of total war. This suggests some of the range of that spectrum, but only a part of it. The point is that I for one am unable to say today where peace begins and war ends. And I certainly cannot use the image of the coin, with peace on one side and war on the other.

We must also, in our new thinking about problems of peace and war, reconsider the purpose of war. We in America are accustomed, largely through happy circumstances of our history, to regard complete victory as the only acceptable outcome of fighting. We won a complete victory in 1783, in 1848, and in 1898. One part of us won a complete victory in 1865. We won complete victories in 1919 and in 1945. And by the good fortune of developments we came to believe that we had won a victory in 1815. We have as a result acquired the tradition of victory. This tradition manifested itself in the attitude of General MacArthur, and those who supported him, toward the war in Korea. But may we not have come to the time when complete victory is impossible? How can you speak of complete victory in a war of atomic weapons? It is at least arguable that complete victory will henceforth be impossible without paying the price of atomic destruction.

It was this issue that was at the heart of the so-called MacArthur controversy in 1951. It is an issue that is going to be with us for some time. It is going to be hard for us to learn that we cannot always have wars come out as we wish, as they did in the past. We may, in this connection, have to rethink our attitude toward our relationship with the enemy. A brilliant historian, Herbert Butterfield, of Cambridge University in England, who is also one of the leading Anglican laymen of our day, has written a book called *Christianity, Diplomacy and War*. In this book, Mr. Butterfield has raised some fascinating questions, particularly about such things as what he calls "the war for righteousness." By this expression he means wars during which all the people of the enemy country are hated and called "little yellow so-and-so's," and even regarded as sinners who must be punished by the victors. He reminds his readers, as a good Christian should, that the punishment of sinners is not something that Christ believed should be left in the hands of men, and suggested that we need to return to Christianity in our thinking about the nature of war.

We must also think a great deal about peace. The search for peace is a hard task. It is easy to say "peace, it's wonderful," but that solves nothing. What price are you willing to pay for peace? What price are the Russian leaders willing to pay for peace? In the past there was a tendency, perfectly natural and understandable, especially among Christians who look toward the Prince of Peace, to assume that most people desire

Joseph E. Johnson

peace and that only a few evil or foolish men fail to desire peace. Is that right? There are eight hundred million people now under the control of men who have rejected Christianity and all other religions, who are materialistic, who insist that the human soul and the after-life are unimportant or nonexistent. Do these men desire peace? And, if so, for what reasons? And if we can find the reasons, how then do we approach them in order to help achieve peace? There is, as far as I know, nothing in the record of the men who have ruled the Kremlin since 1917 that shows they have the same regard for peace and hold the same distaste for war that we do. And yet they are there, and we must deal with them.

The second field in which bold new thought is required is that which students of the problem call the decision-making process. We know much too little today, particularly in the field of foreign affairs, about how decisions are reached, especially in a democracy. I do not mean by this that everyone needs to know the contents of the secret papers that officials consult in making their decisions. I mean that we do need to perfect the decision-making process. Several years ago there was serious criticism in the papers of the way in which what is called the "new military look" was arrived at. Editors and columnists questioned whether men inside the executive branch of the government had any business making a decision of the importance of that one without consulting Congress and the people much more thoroughly than they did. This is an example of the problems involved in the decision-making process. At present, we leave too much to chance, fail to follow orderly processes. There is an old saying in the State Department that policy is made in answer to an incoming telegram. This is not always true, but it is true oftener than it should be. A friend of mine, one of our most distinguished career Foreign Service Officers, now serving abroad as an ambassador, once said: "You know I had to make that decision in twenty minutes and I really ought to have had forty-five!" This illustrates a major problem of our governmental structure.

In considering and developing an understanding of the nature of the decision-making process, we Americans must abandon our belief that solutions can always be found. We have a wonderful phrase: "The difficult we do today, the impossible takes a little longer." That concept has great value in industrial production and in military production, but it is misleading and dangerous when applied to issues as complex as those we face in foreign affairs today. It took from May 1947 until June 1948 to develop the Marshall Plan, and that was a miracle of speed. In our diplomatic history there was one issue, not a major one, which took from 1783

Joseph E. Johnson

to 1911 to settle; it involved the right of Gloucester fishermen to fish in Canadian waters. I go so far as to say that we should not look for solutions of issues in foreign affairs. It has been wisely said that in this field you do not solve problems, you learn to live with them.

We Americans are concerned with this challenge of world peace, and we are responding to it, indeed we have to respond to it. Our government does so, and the citizens try to do so as individuals or as groups. Since we have not thought hard enough so far about the challenge, the responses are many. One group of American people responds to the problem of the atom with the proposal that we must have world government at once. Another group of Americans responds to the problem of a difficult world by saying, "Let's turn back on ourselves and ignore the rest of the world." From world government to isolation the spectrum is complete. I stand just about in the middle of this spectrum. I happen to believe very firmly that our policy as it has been pursued by two administrations since 1945 has been about the best we could have. Some respond in fear, by the fear upon which McCarthy and McCarran have fed. Others respond to boldness, such as that with which President Truman moved when North Koreans invaded South Korea or that which President Eisenhower exemplified when he went before the United Nations General Assembly in December 1953 with his proposal for the peaceful uses of atomic energy. Some respond by a search for panaceas and "gimmicks."

Given the nature of the problem this tremendous range of responses is not unnatural.

For myself, I am not afraid. As a student of American history I have found that examination of the record of our country breeds confidence, hope, and faith. We have met other challenges and met them well when fear was absent. And I would remind you of a phrase from a speech: "The only thing we have to fear is fear itself." Remember the impact of that phrase and the reaction to it on the part of the American people.

In some respects we have met the present challenge well: the development of the United Nations; staying in the United Nations and continued support of it despite strident voices, without considering it the be-all and end-all of our policy; the development of the Marshall Plan; the establishment of the North Atlantic Treaty Organization; leadership of the successful effort to stop aggression in Korea on a collective basis. These are actions of which I think we have reason to be very proud. And looking back on where we were fifteen years ago, we can have pride, mingled with some surprise, in ourselves, in our capacity for response to a challenge.

Joseph E. Johnson

The challenge of emerging nationalism it seems to me we have not met so successfully. We are not yet bold in the areas of activity in which the threat or use of force is not an answer. We have not thought sufficiently about the economic and the psychological, and the political, and the spiritual means of meeting our challenge. We can meet this challenge too. We have the moral, the spiritual and the intellectual qualities, but we must mobilize them all and constantly, for in the atomic age we can not fail.